PRAISE FOR
RUNNING THE
OLD ROAD IN
YELLOWSTONE

"I love this story because it's about being an explorer—a reminder that we can all do this, but most people never get the chance. We all just need a friend to get us moving."

—BILL RODGERS, 4x winner of Boston and NYC Marathons

"This book is like a daily run on the same course. Each page turn is like a new day, on a familiar course, but the nuances discovered along the way are palpable. Each word was like skipping and skimming along a gnarly trail, always taking in the hazards, as well as the beauty, cautious not to miss anything, as each footfall could create a new memory or help us recall one from the past."

—ROY PIRRUNG, ultramarathon and long-distance runner

Running the Old Road in Yellowstone

Tim Norris

》》》 **hatherleigh**

Hatherleigh Press, Ltd.
62545 State Highway 10,
Hobart, NY 13788, USA
hatherleighpress.com

RUNNING THE OLD ROAD IN YELLOWSTONE

Library of Congress Cataloging-in-Publication Data is available.
ISBN: 978-1-961293-27-4

Cover photography by Jacob W. Frank / National Park Service
Printed in the United States

The authorized representative in the EU for product safety
and compliance is Catarina Astrom, Blästorpsvägen 14,
276 35 Borrby, Sweden. info@hatherleighpress.com

10 9 8 7 6 5 4 3 2 1

*For my loving and beneficent wife, Mary Jane, and
for my talented and magnificent sons, Alex and Ansel, and
for Dave and Jennifer Anderson of Colorado Springs,
who cherish Yellowstone and family and each other.*

CONTENTS

PREFACE

Nobody saw it coming. Not the National Weather Service, not the National Park Service, not the Army Corps of Engineers or monitors from local and state governments, not any of more than 40,000 men, women and children living in and around settlements in Park and Carbon counties, from Livingston to Cooke City, Montana and south across the northern boundary of Yellowstone National Park to Mammoth Hot Springs, Wyoming.

On June 13, 2022, tropical air pushing up from Florida collided with a slow-moving cool front from the northwest. The storm and sudden snowmelt unleashed torrents and maelstroms, pumping the Yellowstone River and tributaries to all-time record levels, carving huge gaps into U.S. Highway 89 and sending rock and mud tumbling onto that main route connecting east with west and north with south. The tumult knocked out power, damaged bridges, flooded homes and businesses, polluted drinking water and cut off local communities from supply lines and the outside world. Residents and visitors alike, even the most self-reliant loners, would share collective losses and urgency.

As near as 500 yards above the Gardner River's dramatic slash into the southbound U.S. 89 connecting Gardiner and Mammoth Hot Springs, a rough-and-ready companion route came through unscathed.

The Old Road.

I was not surprised. Even many current Park employees gave no thought to the old dirt-and-gravel wagon road that once carried stage-coaches and buckboards from the train station in Gardiner through

Yellowstone's north entrance to the hotel in Mammoth, where visitors could step into horse-drawn connections to the wider park.

That image of flood damage stays with me. When I came to Yellowstone for the summer season in 2005, I was awash in my own failures and self-doubt. I thought I had sought the Park for work at minimum wage, to pay what I could of child support and fend off creditors and the IRS.

Now, from a distance through time and space, I see photos of bulldozers and dump trucks troweling and smoothing the quirky gravel. Agencies leading the recovery from the floods have gone to work widening the Old Road to two lanes, shoring it up, smoothing it out, plastering much of it in pavement, not for any lasting need of humans and animals but for immediate access. And I expect, for a burst of political reassurance and temporary jobs and, maybe, a tidy profit for a few inflata-bulls, gaming the losses and fears. Easy for me to say, from a distance. Pressure to restore a link was enormous, and the quick work was impressive.

The only bulls I met in Yellowstone were bison, and they were loners. I had to relate. That's where I came from and what I cultivated. Among many hundreds of workers and upwards of four million park visitors that season, I still felt alone. I could find strange comfort in that, and I sought solitude.

When I had very little but hope, the Old Road was part of my salvation. No human habitations allowed. Among the Road's local residents: bison and pronghorn antelope, coyotes and elk, a celebration of birds and insects and small mammals (is that a groundhog? Is that a mole?), I felt a sense of community.

I needed humankind, too, but just then, I didn't want it. I was stepping into a new frontier among a horde of strangers. My lifelong survivor shields were up and active.

I only learned slowly that, even more than money and solace, I was looking for reconstruction. For redemption. I had no idea how or where to look for that.

INTRODUCTION

As a scenic marvel and a getaway, Yellowstone National Park promises the extraordinary: novelty, surprise, grandeur, magic. Its most popular nickname is "Wonderland." Some long-timers call it "Oz." It's also fully grounded, not just atop the massive cone of a simmering volcano but in hard human labor. I've learned that firsthand...and foot.

I lived and worked at Old Faithful in the park and then at Yellowstone Gallery & Frameworks in Gardiner, Montana, across Park Street from the North Entrance and Roosevelt Arch, for just seven months, April to October of 2005. Those months, though, left an indelible mark. Even laced into a work routine, every day seemed new. Facing personal ruin, I heeded the advice that my father recommended until the end of his 92 years, and took those days one at a time.

From color-splashed print coverage and advertising and from sublime and dramatic photoplays over multi-media, days and views in Yellowstone might seem similar, but no two are ever alike. Every geyser and "thermal feature" always comes that way. Every run does, too.

In the presence and present of Yellowstone, as in my many other stops, I did my best to run every other day. Running had rescued me from failures, restored my balance and confidence, fed my imagination, and, here, it took me out among the geysers and pools and terraces of travertine, along tumbling creeks, and onto a network of trails and boardwalks. I even hazarded a couple of riskier runs overland. Underbrush intrudes, fallen trees snag; I came back scratched and frustrated, and I stuck from then on to trammeled or at least half-prepared ground, to the uneven threads of bare earth first beaten by deer and elk, widened by Shoshone, Crow, Blackfeet and Bannocks, the first humans to live among the geysers.

This is ground charted and mapped for the wider world in the early 1800s by, among others, Father Pierre Jean De Smet and Washington Hood of the Army Corps of Engineers.

My feet only know the feel of them. Rocks. Roots. Marsh. Meadow. Clumps of scrub oak and clusters of pine. Smooth stretches stitching the rough patches together into a mapped trail.

In my time in Yellowstone and Gardiner, I kept a daily log of experiences on my laptop, and I'll use those to shore up the story. Running and other exercise also have flavored my life as it unfolds every day.

The physical act of running and the physical place of America's first and greatest national park have at least two key elements in common:

Balance and adventure.

Distance runners, navigators of roads and trails (as opposed to tightly measured oval tracks or circumscribed road courses) find footing in the commonplace and mystery in the unknown, in what waits around the next curve or corner or beyond the next hill or arroyo or bend in the river. And none of them knows exactly how a race or workout or even a casual run will unfold.

Yellowstone percolates with mystery. Even tourists rooted to the Grand Loop and its conjoined sites and walkways discover sights and sounds beyond their imaginations. The action crowd can find not just guided tours but horseback riding and river-running and mountain climbing. And there are the explorers, not just flamboyant or misguided risk-takers but anyone observant and curious and venturesome.

Most runners, in my experience, are born to explore. I like to think that most of them keep exploring, through the glare and fogs, the heights and bogs, the extended plains and pains of everyday existence, to the hope of something better, across that final finish line.

1

INTO THE
WILDERNESS

In more than 40 years of distance running, I had never worried about what was behind me and rarely felt threatened by what was ahead. I ran at my own pace, easy or urgent, confident or cautious, taking each run as it came. Even when, in my training for the New York Marathon in 1978, a dog jumped off a porch and across a lawn in suburban Omaha and took a little piece out of my left knee, I had a route to run. So, I yelled at the owner, who was just sitting in a porch chair on his hind parts and grinning. He never lifted a finger or his ass, and I avoided the temptation to give HIM the finger and kept going. (Not long after, that dog bit a neighbor and was taken in and put down. I would have saved the dog and taken in the owner.) I didn't blame the dog, just the owner, and in those days, I didn't like stopping, even for a red light or a torn knee.

I *do* honor red lights at intersections on city streets and busy roads, but I see those streets as serving both people in machines and people on foot. Years ago in downtown Salt Lake City, I was running across an intersection on State Street, heeding a green light in a crosswalk, when a braking car bumped me, I turned and slapped a palm on its hood as hard as I could. WHAM! I can still see the driver's stunned and bug-eyed face. I gave him one more hard stare and kept running.

The only other time I remember stopping, in peak form, was when I was running a neighborhood route in Milwaukee with my best buddy, a shepherd-lab mix named Carmen, and a pit bull came after her off a porch. I kicked the pit bull in the teeth, wishing I could have kicked the owner. Instead, Carmen and I kept running.

On my last working night in Gardiner, Montana, the northern gateway to Yellowstone, I took a farewell run on (for me) hallowed ground: The Old Road. As I leaned into the third switchback on the road's north-to-south ascent, between Gardiner and Mammoth Hot Springs, Wyoming, something came after me. I was alone, as usual, all-too-aware that the Old Road winds through wild country, with bison and pronghorn antelope nearby and wolves and coyotes and a possible bear in the offing, no canine companion to alert me. To feel nervous, I needed only to glance at warning posters in a few shop windows on Park Street in Gardiner as I walked to work, vivid views of the bloody result of a man whose back had been shredded by a grizzly.

No matter. In any entanglement with terrain or weather or wild-life, I didn't like being bossed or dancing with worry, no matter how practical the warnings were. I *did* love, and still love, what running any course under any conditions always provides: mystery. Sometimes, as my own detective, I happily resolve it. Sometimes I'm the victim. Always, with a road or path playing out in front, I'm the author… author of my own effort, at least.

Now and then, something magical happens. It can also be tragic. On the road that last night, it might have been both. I had been living, and running, on the proverbial and sometimes literal edge. My spring and summer and early autumn here, in the park and just to the north, were over. I had no job ahead, no prospects. I was trying to survive.

Now, in tempestuous darkness, I'm not smiling. As I head up the switchbacks, I know that I would have to clean my rented apartment thoroughly in the morning and pack the Buick and head on out. No job waiting for me. No address of my own. Badly behind on child support. Nothing else I can do besides prepare for what's in front of me right here, right now. Then listen for the rhythms of body and landscape and try to ride them.

Ahead of me, through the swirling dark, the Old Road rises with its ruts and rocks through three switchbacks toward the first high crown of hill. In the dark, I'm running more deliberately and cautiously than usual. Conditions on these mostly uphill five miles are getting worse. Chilling rain pelts me and softens the rocky ground underfoot, clarion of the first snow, and I focus on navigation and memory, trying to anticipate potholes and rocks and roots that could send me to a hard fall.

I've just started that turn into the third switchback when, from the darkness, a siren hits me. From ears to toes, it stops me like a mattress. It seems only a few yards away, but in a flurry of echoes off surrounding rocks I can't tell if it's ahead or behind or, as it seems, all around me.

I stand still, through my own breathing and blood-surge. No, not a siren, a bugle. I turn my ears and I find the source, up the hill to the right. The darkness shifts around something very big.

I listen, hear a slight shifting that must be the wind through wet fur. Vision coalesces around an elongated hulk, capped in a tree of sharp tips.

Bull elk. Five feet tall or more at the shoulder, they can weigh more than 1,000 pounds and run more than 25 miles-an-hour, and their antlers could skewer a family of five. That bugle is a challenge.

My runs are rarely interrupted, especially by animals, though I've swallowed my share of gnats and run through clouds of deer flies and (much better) lightning bugs. I've hopped over snakes and dodged alligators, dodged swooping hawks and owls, side-stepped herds of whitetail deer, even in New Jersey. As for humanity, I stopped, once, in a park in Omaha for a woman cyclist who had just been hit by a car, and I consoled her until the ambulance came.

This bull elk, I'm sure, isn't challenging me. I'm no contest. He's warning any other bull in the area to stay away from his female or females. As I stand, listening, he bugles again, a little closer, and it shivers my ears and my timbers. What could I do? I decide that I'm cold enough and wet enough and tired enough to turn around.

His sound and his stance, though, stay with me. He's not a creature of some insurance company or somebody's cartoon. He's out in it, doing what he can, not just to survive but to live.

Running is not just physical. It is, for lack of a better word, spiritual. Maybe I look to running in the way I look to Yellowstone, as an anodyne to an erratic life; you know, the comforter. The painkiller.

Nothing can blur the written memories, at least, from my daily diary. With them, my time in Yellowstone seems as vivid as last night's windstorm or yesterday's run over dog-prints on a muddy trail in Copp Family Park, Groton, CT.

2
REFUGE

The adventure on the Old Road on my last day in Yellowstone freshened memories of my first day in the park and in Gardiner seven months before.

I was 56 years old, and I was broke and out of work. Also divorced and bankrupt and low on hope, beleaguered by bills, trying to support two young sons, Alex and Ansel, on what charitably could be called "limited income," as in part-time temporary or seasonal income or, for some stretches, none.

I'd been living for more than a year and a half in Baraboo, Wisconsin, home of the Ringling family and Circus World Museum, inhabiting a well-worn double-wide trailer with my mother in a trailer court lavishly named Blackhawk Manor.

My mother, Myra Mae McMillan Norris Furse, and my stepfather, George Furse, had landed there because it gave them a central launch point in summer and fall for the weekend crafts-fair circuit.

I witnessed their move to Baraboo, early in 1986, from their half of a rented duplex on 41st and Center Streets in Milwaukee, the Sherman Park neighborhood, because I was living with them at the time, back from finishing grad school at the University of Oregon. I helped them load the rental truck, and I stayed behind, commuting by bus to a secretarial job at the Milwaukee County Zoo. Some days, after Animal Department meetings, I came home smelling like elephant.

Mom marketed her quilts (she almost gave them away, at a labor rate I once calculated at about 20 cents an hour), and George played and sold his bamboo flutes, painstakingly made in a small shed in all weathers. By hand he bored and smoothed the shafts and fluted the finger holes, and the music of his demonstrations called across town parks and shopping malls and courthouse squares. They lived in the trailer without even mild complaint, and the trees George planted in the yard around it, now a few stories high, splashed them with shadow while the flower gardens they tended garnished the lawns, papering it with color.

The walls of George's heart were paper-thin, too, but the heart inside was big. He left a job teaching high school Spanish in Cleveland to live in the desert and then in the tropics among local people, and he spoke up for them in English-speaking courts, there and here, as a translator. He appeared in the Sauk County Courthouse the day before he died, to translate for a defendant who only spoke Spanish.

On George's last morning, Mom found him curled near the toilet, where he spent too much of his time arduously executing functions routine for most people. Pissing hurt. Shitting hurt more. I never heard him complain. When he stood up to the draft board in Cleveland after Pearl Harbor and told them, respectfully, that as a minister's son he couldn't kill anybody, they sent him to Puerto Rico as an orderly in a hospital. He lost 40 pounds and wasn't released from service until 1946. He said it was one of the great experiences of his life. He married and taught high school Spanish in Cleveland for 30 years and then threw it all over, the cars, the colonial, the wife, to live with the Incas in Peru, learning, among other things, flute-making. He came back to Texas, where he harvested bamboo for his own flutes, and it was there, literally sick at heart, that he first traded Voicespondence tapes with my mother.

He was braver than I'll ever be. He would have done all right, I think, if he had gravitated to, say, Wyoming or Montana. I thought I might do all right out there, too. Seems easier out west for a vagrant to find direction.

When I landed in the trailer, I stuffed my furniture and belongings into a storage locker across the tracks where circus trains had run, south of the Sysco plant, and set my laptop on a table in the kitchen. We had no Internet access, so I had to reserve time on public computers at the Baraboo Library, 30 minutes per customer. Mom, insisting that I take the big bed in the master bedroom, slept in her sewing room.

I couldn't replace George. I could help, clumsily, with a leaky faucet or a stuck door, and I could bring my young sons Alex and Ansel up from Madison on weekends. In the meantime. I canvassed Sauk County on foot and the World Wide Web on fingertips for a job.

Any day, I expected to be called back to newspaper work. I was good! I had won awards! OK, three, but they were GOOD. Put that in your cup of coffee and stir it.

Every day, I was disappointed. I spent part of each day in personnel offices filling out job applications and scanning online job sites (especially JournalismJobs.com), another part copying my stories and sending packets of resumes and clips to newspapers needing writers.

I also desperately needed income. I took part-time seasonal jobs at near-or-below minimum wage that most people avoided, cleaning the many public toilets at Devils Lake State Park, cutting tee boxes and grooming sand traps at Baraboo County Club, taking telephone catalog orders in a small booth at Lands' End in Dodgeville. After more than a year, when my second Lands' End winter season closed, I started casting about for work in places I loved. If I'm doomed to a purgatory of "temporary and seasonal," I might as well spend my off-hours in a heavenly place.

Yellowstone topped the list. I visited the park first in 1961, at age 12, when the family camped at Jenny Lake down in the Tetons under a big yellow tent, took food from a Coleman cooler and light from a Coleman lantern and then ventured north to the Big Gig for a whirlwind tour of the Grand Loop. I remember hearing on a portable radio that Roger Maris of the New York Yankees was battling teammate Mickey Mantle for the all-time single-season home run record. As we waited in the Mercury station wagon in a long line at Yellowstone's South Entrance, black bears padded right up to our open windows, looking for food. And then...

The geysers! The bubbling pools of hot water and mud! The sulfurous smell of rotten eggs but even more, the ambrosia of lodgepole pine and Douglas fir! Waterfalls at every turn! Herds of bison and elk, pronghorn antelope, eagles and sandhill cranes! Burgers and ice cream and cool souvenirs galore!

The West called to me, too. By day, the great rises and stretches beyond the Missouri River appear almost too bright, sun glare spanking off rocks and shimmering on flats and roadways. At night, in the vast darkness hiding the mountains and foothills and arroyos and plateaus and their twisted and tortured and multi-hued geologies, lights clump. Ranch houses, truck stops, oil refineries, small towns. I had forgotten how to look for them. I've wondered, at times, what light led the first miners to their grubstakes, here.

I know what's led me back: a glimmer of what they brought in surplus. Hope. Foolhardiness. The usual dreams, standard-issue. Or because, when you're lost, any place familiar can be better than no place. Better than the road.

Now, armored with experience, I imagined guiding tours, writing blurbs, helping animals.

Get in line. The National Park Service demands credentials far beyond mine, and non-profits such as the Yellowstone Foundation boast legions of passionate naturalists and teachers and authors with park savvy and connections, eager to lecture and guide.

One outfit didn't care much about contacts or credentials. Xanterra Parks & Resorts operates hotel and food services in Yellowstone and other big national parks, and it took applications online. It hired by mail, too. Minimum wage, sure, but also food and lodging, out of the paychecks. I had one brief phone call (to see if I were breathing, I suppose) and then a letter came: I was in! Sorry, Mom, but otherwise I'd be living off your Social Security, and the Child Support people would go nuts.

I drove a well-beaten 1992 Buick sedan from Wisconsin across Minnesota, past flat farms into uplands along the Mississippi River, across the Missouri and past the Badlands into more Western landscapes, through the Black Hills of South Dakota and on to Wyoming, and I kept notes of the trip, in present tense, on my laptop. Here's an example:

In Dayton, Wyoming, I gas the car, mail cards to Alex and Ansel (my young sons back in Wisconsin). A sign outside the Branding Iron Café declares Good Luck Seniors (May, graduation). I'm a senior of the other stripe, the silver-streaked skunkish kind, and I need some of that luck.

The Tongue River is running high, lapping at weedy banks, on a turn through Connor Battlefield State and Historic Site. The place is neglected and overgrown. I drive past information signs and picnic tables. The monument celebrates Patrick E. Connor, Union General in the Civil War later assigned to Salt Lake City, where he captained construction of Fort Douglas. Fearful of actual and rumored attacks on white settlements and both issuing and following orders, Connor oversaw troops whose attacks sent hundreds of Native Americans to death, starvation and bleak reservations. No smile and salute here, sir.

Sign on the edge of town:

(Highway) 14 Closed When Flashing, Return to Dayton

Not flashing. Up into the catamounts, accompanied from the in-car audio by Aaron Copland's "Rodeo" and "Billy the Kid." Hello, Big Horn Mountains. U-turning up the switchbacks. Up from 14 to 212 at Cody.

An hour or so in, a light snow peppers the windshield. It thickens. As I approach Burgess Junction, at some 9,000 feet, I plant the Buick in the tracks of a semi-trailer truck just ahead. Near noon, now. The Junction advertises restrooms and a café. Both are closed. No lunch or relief for me.

I step behind a building and pee the way the bears do. My shepherding semi-trailer is long gone, but I manage to navigate Bear Tooth Pass. On the backslopes the snow plays out. Finally, I see a wood sign with familiar lettering and park service arrowhead.

YELLOWSTONE NATIONAL PARK

Glory be!

Like L. Frank Baum's mythical Oz, Yellowstone can be broken roughly into four quadrants, defined somewhat by geography and history but mostly by entrances: North at Gardiner; East through Greybull and Cody; South up from Jackson, Wyoming; West through West Yellowstone, Montana. The oddball fifth and least frequented entrance is the one I've used.

The northeast portal is the simplest and most rugged, a log building extending wings to booths for coming and going. As I present my paperwork on the inbound, an odd and funny moment: the older woman ranger thinks she has seen me before. Xanterra employee; haven't I already been through here? I assure her that I haven't, say something such as "Good-looking guy, though, huh?" and both she and the younger woman ranger laugh. Maybe I'm generic. I'm relieved to be getting in free.

Sun shoots through banks of dark clouds, combing the rugged mountains, ribboning the broad riverbeds, and I descend into the Hayden Valley. Spectacular! The animals I see, bunching and grazing, are bison. The road is wide open.

I'm off the diary now. I remember passing through Tower, across to Norris, up through Mammoth Hot Springs.

This is the start of the adventure. I arrive to a night at the Absaroka Motel in Gardiner, a town sprawled along the Yellowstone River at the north entrance. My sons and I had stayed in this motel on our first visit three years before, and I remember the manager as alternately brooding and frantic. He is still the manager, and he is still brooding and frantic. Things will improve, he says, when his summer help gets in from colleges in the U.S. and in Eastern and Central Europe and from Mexico or Colombia. I watch the last TV I am likely to see for months, take the last shower in privacy.

Before the shower, I stop at the headquarters for Targhee National Forest and ask about local running trails. I am directed to one along the river's north side, accessed from the parking lot of the Latter-Day Saints Church. I'm there!

The trail has been cut into the side of the river's gorge, and is rough, rocky and hilly. Aware that I am now at least five thousand feet higher than usual, I wait to be hammered by oxygen debt. Along the way, I scan the upslope repeatedly for bears and other carnivores.

What nearly does me in, though, is a vegetable.

Snowmelt cascades down the canyon walls in ribbons and rivulets in several places and, farther up, in tumbling creeks. Early on, two vigorous freshets have allowed deciduous trees to take root and, dodging them, have covered some of a series of rocks I might otherwise use for crossing. In the second of these shaded alcoves, I spot a flat stone amidst the rush and land on it.

Big mistake. The rock is covered with moss or algae and is as slippery as petroleum jelly on a bowling ball. My right foot skids and flies into the air, the left leg buckles and slams shin-first into another rock, and I fall heavily sideways. I land on my right shoulder, my head inches from a larger and sharper stone. I lie there just a second, startled, relieved, aggravated, and then bounce up, as I have learned to do, and find dry footing and resume running. I'm aware that my left shin is bleeding, but the adrenalin dulls any pain. From then on, all things considered, the run isn't bad. The scenery, even as I scan it for bears, is breathtaking.

The wound is a superficial gash in two streaks, below the knee to the shin. I soap it heavily in the shower and spray on Bactine borrowed from the office and feel OK.

The next morning, limping just a little, I am processed through the personnel office located in a massive concrete structure still carrying the logo of the Yellowstone Park Company, now leased by Xanterra. The assignment sheet reads:

General Help, Geyser Grill, Old Faithful

I can take solace, not in the tourist-magnet but because Old Faithful is where college roommate and long-time friend Dave Anderson and his wife Jennifer and their children and grandchildren convene each year, up from Colorado Springs. They would reappear, I figured, over the July 4th holiday, the only familiar faces I expected to see.

With two sets of clothes (pants, shirts, aprons) and a jaunty black baseball cap lettered above the brim with YELLOWSTONE and along the right temple with STAFF, I point the Buick toward the entrance cabin and up the asphalt New Road from Gardiner to Mammoth, toward survival.

3
BITTERROOT

Yellowstone surrounds me. I am an employee, now, April 15, 2005, not a visitor. So much seems strange. As I drive south on the west leg of the Grand Loop, very little looks familiar. Maybe it's the eye of this beholder, fogged by doubt, drooping with age and misadventure.

I first brought my sons Alex and Ansel to the park in the late '90s, and we hit the high spots. A photo album I put together shows Ansel staring at three elk from a few yards away at a National Park Service building in Gardiner, and Alex posing in front of a wood sign in Mammoth pointing to Norris, and both of them silhouetted against the plumes of Old Faithful and the sprawl of Yellowstone Lake.

Coming south from Mammoth, I'm passing over a viaduct through the great canyon called Golden Gate, between Bunsen Peak and Terrace Mountain, and along a retinue of oddly shaped rocks that haunt me: the Hoodoos.

Ghostly white, they are boulders of travertine limestone tumbled down from Terrace Mountain, lined up as if waiting for action.

This place is a world of its own. This is a kingdom, I would soon learn, of phantoms, drifting on clouds and columns and billowing coruscations of steam. Some of the phantoms are expectation, the many thousands of calendars and promotional images of Yellowstone and, especially, of a single seminal geyser, Old Faithful. O.F. is modest in dimension, and I'd argue that at least a dozen geysers within the park are bigger and more interesting performers, starting just down the boardwalk with Grand, Castle and Riverside. But, in ethos, Old Faithful is iconic and titanic.

I check in at a company table in Old Faithful Lodge and follow a walking map from the hump and outwash of the great geyser, past the post office, through a stand of lodgepole pine and across the busy Loop to an outpost of a hidden world: Bitterroot.

It's a dark brown dormitory, screened from traffic and vacationers by curtaining pines. My room is on the second floor; it is not my own. I discover a roommate, about my age: David McElwain of Mississippi. Large guy, comes in wearing a cap showing a springbok, colorful antelope of South Africa that serves as a national symbol. McElwain says he just came from working construction there.

Our room is part of a mirrored pair, the other hosting two young collegians, with a shared bathroom, toilets and shower in between. My father, a Navy veteran of WW II, seemed entirely comfortable in similar quarters (YMCA, golf courses, tennis clubs) changing and showering among strangers. Not me. I have trouble stepping to crowded urinals or doffing duds in any public place.

When our employer's shifts don't mix and the co-residents are gone, I am happy (and relieved) to change into shorts, shirt and shoes and escape to the nearest trail, beaten through nearby pines toward a rocky up-crop. The air smells clean and gives me a tingle.

The best trail waits just ahead. Here's how I find the Old Road.

I have stepped into the National Park Service personnel office at Mammoth Hot Springs, asking about job openings, trying to escape fast-food purgatory, thinking I can find a better fit. Writer? Tour guide? Bison wrangler? Melanie Moroney, the amiable office manager, scans openings and says she's sorry, nothing now. I can fill out a general application. Sure. Done that many times.

Then, under her sympathetic gaze, I confess my confinement to park boundaries, and she mentions a way to leave my car among the buildings of the old military post and walk to Gardiner, saving me the $20 park entrance fee. "See that Yield sign there?" she says, pointing across the entrance road and its grassy median. "You'll see a path just beyond it. Just take that up and over the hill and you'll hit the Old Road. You can walk right down into town." The road ends, she says, at the ranger station, and nobody there will so much as say boo to me.

That initial hill proves steep, and my effort to sling a plastic bag (needed to deflect rain from banks of dark clouds looming to the north) filled with my books and papers over my shoulder fails. The bundle slides off my shoulder.

The road itself is twin tracks of dirt, easy on the feet, with a median of patchy fescue and blue-bunch, tumbling down from Mammoth's heights and swerving around foothills. As I leave the steaming alabaster shelf of the hot springs behind, the first big turn brings a breathtaking view of grassy fields climbing to pine-crowned heights, the tumbling Gardner River, more fields set before more rounded hills rising to higher hills and, beyond, the snow-capped Absaroka range and the crown of Electric Peak. Even under a glowering sky, this is a view most commonly frozen for calendars.

Who, I wonder, first cut this road along the hips of the hills? Was it the only access until the '20s, when drivers of the oncoming swarm of automobiles and buses and trucks pushed for a carpet of sterner stuff?

As the road descends, I imagine what trappers and prospectors and other pioneers faced as they blazed their own trails…or followed paths already tamped or hewn by native Americans and by animals. As I round a bend, I spot a pronghorn, rubbing its spiked horns on a sage bush. It starts to raise its head, spots me and sprints away.

The walk down is five miles. The walk back up seems a little longer. But I have a few snacks and a movie disc in hand, and their plastic bag swings lightly. Running this route, I tell myself, will be FUN. Occasional discomfort aside, I'm happy to be here, happy to be (with the next step) right here, right now.

Finding my way to "right here" can be a carousel or a kaleidoscope, new jobs, lost jobs, new loves, lost loves, successes and failures and fresh chances. In the detail and urgency of "right now," running acts as a salve and, maybe, an earthy and Earthly salvation.

That's what I'm here for: redemption. Mind, spirit, bank account. This road looks hard and rocky. It's saying, "Show me what you got." Not much? We'll see.

4
ON THE LINE

Before my first shift in the Geyser Grill, April 16, 2005, I take my first run inside the boundaries of Yellowstone Park. The day is cool and sunny. Across the park's 3,471 square miles and even along the restricted and traffic-trammeled Grand Loop, I would seem to have a lot of choices. What I lack is a map, a guide to overland trails. I trot from the dorm across the highway to the boardwalk circling Old Faithful.

The slightly elevated wooden walkway (in some stretches recycled plastic) turns west and then north into the Upper Geyser Basin and into a gentle self-generated breeze that smells of sulfur and pine, I see, for the first time, the tantrum of Beehive Geyser and then the siliceous sinter (geyserite) parapets of Castle Geyser and the pool of Grand Geyser nestled into an embrace of rocks and pines, and I feel my spirit lifting.

C'mon, I have a job, food and clothing, a place to rest my head and a new world to explore. Even a little worried about work, even laboring a little, I feel a positive charge. Turn the page! Next chapter!

Next morning the protagonist and conflict are clear. First day of work. How many times have I marched (and staggered) through that drill? Tumbled into that rabbit hole? Time to step (not stride) onto another new scale and test my measure.

Most new workers anywhere face the need to learn quickly, both the detailed demands of a particular job and the mysteries of a culture. Every workplace has its particular routines, and most outfits provide some kind of employee manual with descriptions and expectations, do's and don'ts and don't-evers. Often as not, the type and degree of enforcement is an open question, but instant firing hangs overhead like the Sword of Damocles.

For a newbie, the wild card is relationships, with bosses and co-workers, customers and clients, overseers and regulators, officials and sources. In a first day in newsrooms, I always found comfort in the first assignment, an immediate and familiar challenge. I knew what I was doing, and I reaped the reward. Good story! I was considered a "professional," trained and experienced in the field, and I had the evidence: clips. My published work. Clips, after all, are permanent... at least in microfilm and -fiche and digital files. Even if a prospective boss doesn't know whether the clips are heavily edited and rewritten (I never offered one that wasn't entirely mine, and I took pride in that), the first two or three assignments are proof...or poof.

In newsrooms, I usually passed muster. Until the muster changed and I didn't. Then I stepped into various spans of temporary work, every job with its own immediate demands. Most learning didn't come on a "curve." First day as a secretary in the offices of, for instance, a financial firm and a manufacturer and a zoo. First day as a telephone order-taker in a catalog place, as a numbers scanner and then a medical records assistant in a corporate office, as part of a grounds-keeping crew on a golf course. Just a little slack, and then we've gotta have it now, now, NOW!

I always took comfort in the thoughts of the great John Dewey, whose central lesson was "learn by doing." Yessir. As he knew, "doing" takes all kinds of doing. Learn by enduring. Yellowstone, surviving millions of years atop a volcano, brought the lessons home.

Maybe routines give us momentary refuge. Burger-shuffling shouldn't be tough to learn, just uncomfortable to endure. Not as bad as typing from dictation or adding figures in columns all day long or holding a sign out to traffic, but almost free of challenge or stimulation. Remember the paycheck. Consider the public service. Think positive!

In my green work shirt and black cap with YELLOWSTONE across its crown, I report for duty at the Geyser Grill, north end of the Snow Lodge. It's cool outside, almost too warm inside. Or am I just nervous? I meet Ron and Ole, my bosses, and they show me downstairs to a small room for employees, with its row of lockers and a time clock. They hand me a timecard and invite me to slide it into the wall-mounted Simplex machine and listen for (and feel) the "chunk" of the time stamp.

Punched in! I headed up narrow back stairs to the action.

Will this job punch me out? The last time I took fast-food orders was 40 years ago, 1966, as a "curb boy" at Sky-Way drive-in, Akron, Ohio. The place was owned and run by a generous family appropriately named Large. Stupendously good onion rings, and the best burgers ever. I was a junior in high school. From a central counter and kitchen in a blockhouse, the Sky-Way lot fanned out like a baseball field, and we were dispatched to "right field," "center," or "left," to drop numbered cards on windshields.

We did not wear roller skates, but sometimes in winter we pirouetted on ice. During breaks, I warmed my hands by taking a burger in each, and then my stomach by eating them.

The Geyser Grill more closely mimics the familiar corporate fast-food layout pioneered by the McDonald brothers before Ray Kroc stole it for his larger chain. I started as a line-runner, schlepping food from cooks to customers, and as a lobby-cleaner. If I pass, they'll move me to an order station.

A few days later, off-duty, I am resting on a bench against the Old Faithful Lodge and Xanterra's employee rec center between working rounds of a split shift. Through the wood frame of the porte-cochere angled out from the wood-walled Lodge, I can see knots and tongues of steam rising gently from Old Faithful.

The geyser is simmering between gigs. Cars and vans and campers and trucks and SUVs heading out onto Yellowstone's Grand Loop Highway cast flickering headlights through brindled spears of dead lodgepole pine, torched in the firestorms of 1988, and across the tips of hundreds of bright green seedlings that found light and life when flames seared the seed cluster at the top of each tree. Those saplings have pushed resolutely upward in the years since, carpeting Yellowstone in verdant emerald. Behind me, three young women from Taiwan, co-workers in the Yellowstone hospitality trade, walk toward a weekly open mic in the recreation center, singing a rock ballad in Cantonese.

At the Geyser Grill, I have landed at the end of food chutes (and, in social terms, the food chain). I'll be fielding burgers and hustling orders, index fingers stabbing at menu choices on an IBM flat screen, the rest of me scurrying around in the lulls to sweep floors and restock paper goods and plastic ware, kiddie meals and cup racks, adult ales and ketchup dispensers.

Customers will step up, expecting what everyone expects (demands?) from fast food, thanks to Ray Kroc's transformation of the McDonald brothers' golden-arch drive-in into a global profit machine and mechanical paradigm. But that expectation is not limited to the drive-up-drive-thru.

In far slower and better restaurants, with food provided by master chefs and their disciples, those with taste and/or money expect the same from servers: ease and mastery of the menu, a relaxed and friendly face. I try to smile with the best of them. I want to give these people a break, and to give myself one, too.

In that role we are not quirky individuals with personal histories and grievances and opinions; we are servants of the system, trading work for pay. The best servers are also artists, taking orders by memory, serving 20 or more at a time, remembering what you wanted on a visit three months before. But I'm trying to pound spikes on a metaphorical rail line, here, with spavined fingers.

Three order screens start as a barrage of electronic rectangles, each with its product. Two double bacon cheeseburgers, five fries, three kids' lunches, a buffalo burger, two Cokes and a lemonade and, oh, can I have an Old Faithful Ale?

Hit the right buttons NOW! My fingers stipple and stumble. I glance back at the chutes and the cooler and down at the kids' meal bags lined up under the counter, Tootsie Roll pops in place, yawning open for hot food. Keep SMILING!

The rest of me stumbles into the scan-and-grab for burgers and fries at the end of metal chutes and drinks at the spigot or in the cooler and any unusual order. In idle or urgent moments, the lobby plays the wild card. Clean the tables, on and under! Restock the condiments! Swipe off the dribbles! Hey, a customer! Get your ass back to the counter!

By the end of the first week, I can navigate the screens fairly quickly and, in free moments, grapple with table washes and under-table clean-ups and mustard and ketchup and mayonnaise spigots and pickle and onion bins and run to the basement for supplies. But this is late April, and visitors are just starting to line up.

One morning I found myself bent over ugly cleaning drains with a Chore-Boy, pushing until my hands hurt. I guess I can take some satisfaction from feeding the urgent public and leaving a clean drain, but I want to do better than $6.10 an hour.

My first paycheck, after two weeks, minus the room-and-board and Social Security and other applicable taxes, is $63. But we don't always get what we hope for, or what we work for, either.

5
PANIC GEYSER

On the second day of work, coming back from a 45-mph drive to Mammoth Hot Springs to open an account in the Yellowstone Federal Credit Union, I run into a "bison block."

Veterans and newcomers alike know the view. A herd of western buffalo is shuffling south on the highway and jamming traffic with their shaggy heads and derrieres and cute little tan calves. I am going to be late for my first training session. If I'm fired, then what?

Employees enter the Snow Lodge through an unmarked basement door into a warren lined with pipes and vents, leading to a door marked "Employees Only" on the right and a steep stairway on the left. If this is Wonderland and the white rabbit is hollering "I'm late, I'm late, for a very important date," what would Alice do? Take a chill pill? Nibble the "shrink" side of the caterpillar's magic mushroom and sneak in small, then nibble the "grow?" If I didn't nibble enough, would anyone notice?

I learn, later, that this tunnel and its connections are known as the GUG, the Geyser Under Ground, a hidden world of work. We are not going to dance among the souvenirs.

I nestle my copy of John Steinbeck's *East of Eden* into a locker, stick my first weekly punch card into the time clock and slide it back in the book, head upstairs to the action. I step up to the shift boss, ready for angry censure.

I get a blank face, then a quizzical "Wha...?" The employee roster, I discovered, includes another Tim. On the schedule sheet, I had read his name and hours as mine.

I'm two hours early.

I also learn that my doppelganger has claimed "Tim." I will be "Timothy." The name belongs, among other things, to a kind of grass and a biblical chapter, but the name is not my favorite, though it's better than "Timmy." In my childhood, I was taunted as a tip-toer, thanks to Beatrix Potter's Timmy Tiptoes. The formal Timothy, seemingly more adult, suffered from a more recent pop song by that name, in which Timothy is, among other things, a cannibal.

Maybe Tim will quit, and I can reclaim the nickname. Trying to be friendly, I ask the other Tim about the work, and he says, "I hate fast food! I forgot how much I hated it."

Timothy, Timothy, I say to myself, what have you done?

Work looms, an afternoon shift. The morning is cool, sunny and inviting. In the Old Faithful Visitor Center, I have told a ranger, as hikers here are encouraged to do, that I am going running on the trail to Lone Star Geyser. Don't go alone, she advised me. And don't run. For lack of a partner (preferably a cute and bright and funny woman) with a similar pace, and out of a determination to keep running until I can't anymore, I disobey on both counts. The ranger says, "Grizzlies don't like to be surprised. And they sometimes go after anything running."

Oh, and have a nice time.

I riff through a few bear stories: the day-hiker who surprised a female grizzly and her cubs near Lake Village and took four bloody furrows down his back, the overnighter shredded near his campsite on White Lake by a bear attracted to his foodstuffs, the photographer who missed his last closeup of eyes, nose and teeth. Never mind that many more visitors to Yellowstone die from drowning or scalding or suicide.

That day, not wanting to vanguard the victims list in 2005, I wimp out, instead reprising the main boardwalk and adjoining trail from Old Faithful to Biscuit Basin. I warn clusters of camera-toters with "on your left!" miss a Grand Geyser eruption by minutes and pass two of my favorite and at that moment placid geysers: Solitary and Spiteful.

That's often described me, lately. I might not appear that way, sitting at this same table night after night in Old Faithful Lodge with my laptop, surrounded by diners, watching Old Faithful through the wavy glass. But I don't have much to say to these people, or to the fellow workers I sit near in the EDR (Employee Dining Room).

I always have been a work-in-progress, needing adjustment, but why would anyone else care? Shut up, action steps, turn the page! Wait, is that a stain of Chinese and India ink? No, just my own spill. I also take comfort in isolation, but no one, I'm starting to learn, can endure without human connection.

Desperate for work, repeatedly turned down, increasingly avoiding society, muttering with impatience at drivers who crawl or race or move without signaling and even at my 82-year-old mother, who for the better part of the last two years has given up most of her modest comforts to feed me, I can be a pain in my own butt.

Looping back at the basin near a piping pool, I approach a tattooed, woolen-capped, much-pierced group of young Goths as one of them, wired to satellite radio, announces, "Dude, I just heard (a rock musician, name unclear) shot himself!" The unfortunate dude, a celebrity in another dimension, is as unknown to me as the asshole who threw the first beer bottle or can into Morning Glory Pool.

I get back to Bitterroot and find the shower in use, so I turn to the General Store for comfort: a pint of Bacardi, a Pepsi mixer, a Hostess cherry pie. There goes my spending money.

6

A GUIDE AT GEYSER

Friday, late shift lobby, and a bout with Bob.

The chief potentate of the Geyser Grill's lobby is known as "Reverend Bob," or "Preacher Bob," for his frequent allusions to salvation and the role of God in his own life. On that account, I would never say him nay. He is also known, sotto voce, as "Crazy Bob," maybe for his enthused intensity and for his vivid stories of past adventures (some violent) and solitary wanderings. Not crazy. Just riding a horse of his own. I've found most eccentrics appealing. They fight on the front lines in a war against conformity.

Stop, though. If I'm going to put in seven or eight thankless, back-pinching, knee-pounding hours wiping tables, picking up loose (and used) straws and fries and bits of gnawed meat and bun, shifting bulging trash bags to the dumper, sweeping and mopping floors, keeping stocks of cups and lids and onions and pickles and napkins and ketchup and little plastic-cupped creamers up to Hoyle, I am not going to put up with possessive, holier-than-thou shit from (not-a-boss-but) a co-worker.

Truthfully, I reacted more in our blow-up not to what he said but how he said it. Happened (and still does) with my second ex-wife. Happened with my boss in Kankakee; happened with another of my bosses (I had at least four) in Yuma, two newspaper jobs in my over-age-50 desperation days. Fired, twice. We could debate the causes all day (blame to them, blame to me), but I'm happy to be free of those managers and those disheartening enlistments.

My patience DOES hit walls. When Bob comes at me, as I am arranging the plastic salt and pepper shakers and a comment card with its little pencil on top of the napkin dispenser on a freshly cleaned table, with, "No, NO, not that way!" my right knee twinges in that particular "this is aimed at your balls" manner that signals trouble. Instead of the parry and thrust, I simply swear. I start with, "Well, John told me…" "NO," he says, loudly. "I had training with…and he names some patrician trainer unknown to me…and she taught me how to do it. Like THIS!"

OK, Bob. Fuckyoufuckyoufuckyou! I think that, but I say, "Well, SHIT, who the hell's calling the shots here?" A couple at a nearby table overhear us. They smile at me. Reformed restaurant workers?

Bob leaves the area. When he comes back, he says, first, "Here's why," and shows me that doing it John's way can lead to comment cards sliding down the backs of napkin dispensers and onto the floor. OK, so I say, "Well, that makes sense." Then he says, "I don't care what everyone else says, you're OK with me." He says this, in the next few minutes, three times.

I don't want to be OK with you, Bob. I want you to go away, get scabies or shingles, and suffer. A minute later I relent and just hope he goes away. Which he does. Turns out his shift is over. I don't even have to say, "Take a hike," because that's what he does as a pastime. He invites people on 20 or 30-mile hikes, and then he tells the story of his two bad knees and the metal pin in one of his legs, and I just want to truss him up in a super suit and throw him into the Grand Canyon of the Yellowstone. On national TV. "Let's see you hike outta THERE, you motherfucker!" I'd call down to him, and the echoes off the canyon walls, echoes of my words and of his bony form hitting various stony outcrops, would be especially satisfying.

I realize that this kind of reaction is my Achilles heel. What someone says should always matter more than how he or she or any person says it. I could also learn just to shut up and listen a little, the way I do running in the woods.

At the moment, I'm too busy to consider that. Maybe I'm stuck in this moment; maybe I'm freed by it. But, for the first time in all of my working years, I start to think about the process, about the workflow, about my part in it.

I start to find an opening, to find some light.

I watch Mariska work, her red hair (color not natural) tied in braids today. She moves like a dancer, somewhat the way my friend Irene, Choy Leng Lo, from Yuma days down at the Mandarin Garden, moves in her waitress work. She could handle 30 tables a time, and she kept all orders in her head.

Mariska is from the Czech Republic, I think, or maybe Poland. No, that's right, she's Czech. She told me about her home, in an agricultural flatland. And she is methodical, and thorough, unlike me. She sweeps under every table, every time. Seats are always polished, napkin holders always set perfectly in the center (or center rear) of tables, pencils and comment cards straight and inviting. Every crumb is toweled up. And, in her care, no napkin holder ever shows its naked internal steel; no container is ever left empty of onions, or tartar sauce packets, or ketchup and mustard; no dispenser ever answers a press of the handle with sluggishness and air; no trash container ever burps back a wrapper or soda straw. Whatever the need is, she is (gracefully) ON it. And when the blabby thespian dodderer, Greg, needs me to dump ice into the dispenser above the soft drink machine, she asks to watch so she can learn how. She is lovely, and eager, and earnest, youth's most powerful and enduring qualities. And anyone working with her feels that he or she has an ally.

OK, I can't speak for them. I'm always glad to see her there. And I do not have a crush on her. I don't (he insisted, in his dotage) get those anymore.

7
HOUSEKEEPING

Today, in the Geyser Grill, I almost lose control. A young female co-worker snaps at me when I take an order for a hot dog. "We're OUT of hot dogs!" she barks. "Don't take any more orders for hot dogs! We TOLD you that!"

I didn't remember anyone telling me that, and I'm embarrassed to say that I don't remember the co-worker's name either, just that she's from Texas. Villains should have colorful names. Maybe hers is Sue or Mary or Debbie, or Brunhilda, not that there's anything wrong with that.

Regardless, this is a co-worker. This is not a boss. What do I do, quietly take her aside (nothing "quiet" is possible in that setting, you understand) and say, "Excuse me, but I won't be talked to in that tone?" Or, right there, say, "You can take the next hot dog and ram it up your..." No. Not what a nice lad would do. So, I fume. And smolder. And decide to forget it. I almost do.

Meanwhile, on the lunch break, I am ushered into the Employee Dining Room, the EDR. It's belowdecks in the Snow Lodge, out of public view, and we're invited to eat breakfast there before work or lunch on our half-hour breaks. The eggs and potatoes and mystery meat can be a little bland, but the food is better than I expect. Good salads. Yogurt and fresh fruit. Milk and juice and coffee.

Trying to avoid small talk on this mid-April morning, I look for a table in the corner and bring my latest book, just now *East of Eden*, John Steinbeck's sprawling update of Cain and Abel, transposed to the California lettuce fields.

A few minutes later, a co-worker from the Grill named Michael sits down across from me and looks up from an epic poem to share his dreams of acting, directing, and film making. We talk about Broadway shows and their current wallow. Songs sound the same. Dances look the same. Mass-produced commerce. He touts the classic musicals, and I mention that I've done *Music Man* (chorus) and Gilbert and Sullivan's *Pirates of Penzance* (chorus) and *Mikado* (chorus, though I DID audition for Nankipoo, the tenor lead, and hit the high notes). I could also refer (though I don't) to *Oklahoma* and *West Side Story* (pit orchestra). I played in the pit at Summit High School in New Jersey for *Peer Gynt* (you know, "Hall of the Mountain King" and all that) by Edvard Grieg, where my sister Sarah had a starring role, and in another pit at the University of Oregon for the two-act opera double *Pagliacci* and *Cavalleria Rusticana*. But I don't mention those. "Wow, Gilbert and Sullivan!" he says to my surprise.

A few other strangers clap down trays nearby. Then RJ from Utah (or rather, from California via Utah, a very different thing) leans in, imposing himself.

Here's the kind of guy I usually disparage as a "Cheerful Charlie," a guy unable to suppress his inner toastmaster. This morning he's piping away about falling through the floor of a cabin bathroom and being left hanging from a toilet, and about a former buddy, a tour guide who liked to toke up, or to stay toked up. "We're up on (Something-or-Other) Ridge," he's saying, to an enthused audience, "and I take a step on the downslope and fall down a crack, 20, 25 feet. I'm wedged in down there, trying to get my breath back, and Barlow comes up to the opening and says, "Well, better call maintenance.'"

All right, so I envy the hell out of this guy, me of more modest adventures who can't remember the punch line to more than one joke. One I told to my roommate the other day, inspired by something he said, and now I've blanked on the whole joke. Oh, yeah, it was Dad's joke about Canadians. "Two guys are sitting in a bar, and the smaller guy says, 'Canadians? They're nothing but hookers and hockey players.' The bigger guy glowers, leans in and says, 'My *sister* is from Canada.' And the smaller guy says, 'Yeah? What team does she play for?'"

Michael will be starting his junior year at a Montana university, majoring in theater and film; RJ, it turns out, minored in theater at a state school in California. He will, he says, be doing five minutes of standup comedy in this summer's Old Faithful talent show (workers at the park's five other main sites will put on their shows, too, he says, and the five best acts from each will qualify for the big finale later in the summer). He offers a bit of doggerel lampooning the fare in the EDR as a threat to human life, but I'm not about to write it down and fan his ego, so I've lost it. It WAS pretty funny. Damn him.

Looking for solitude after work and avoiding the dorm, I take refuge in the Old Faithful Lodge, a log building on the east edge of the circular boardwalk, rustic cabins beyond. I sit near a small fireplace south of a snack-and-coffee line and pull out a dated *New Yorker*.

Then a face leans in, and I lift my head from an article on the revival of photorealism. The face shows blue eyes with a little mascara and black hair with an auburn tint and light skin moderately pancaked and belongs to young Veronika from Slovakia, newly arrived, to whom, after she mentioned arriving alone, my roommate David McElwain had said, "You won't be alone for long."

Veronika and I do not talk about romance. We talk about needing sleep, and about avoiding bears and bison. Goodbye. Take care.

When I get back to Bitterroot, Dave tells me that he's taken a good-paying construction job down in Georgia. He packs his kit and leaves in his truck early the next morning, handshake and good luck, mate. I still share a bathroom but, hey, the room is mine! Alone at last.

As I reenter the dorm three days later, climb the stairs, turn the corner, approach the step downward into my part of the place, I find a notice taped to my door. It's *Treasure Island's* black spot on a room-of-one's-own:

> *YOU MAY BE GETTING A ROOMMATE. Arrivals for the Park will happen in the next few days. Please make room and make your new roommate feel welcome. See your RC or Personnel Manager if you have questions.*

Below that management has printed a vacant-eyed, clip-art smiley face coughing out a balloon carrying the words "No whiners!"

Or…what? If a runner whines alone in the woods, is he really making a sound?

8
COMING TO TERMS

Fast food is an exercise in supply, cleanliness, and efficiency. A quartermaster would do well in this business. But fast food has no soul. It has no objective beyond meeting demand and steering clear of health code violations and acting pleasant, shaving the financial margins as closely as possible. Which means $6.10 an hour for the likes of me, and for Linnon from Detroit and James from New York and Laura from back east somewhere, seduced by the promise of a raise of between 25 cents and 75 cents an hour if we come back next year or stay the winter, the way our departed co-worker Athena did, gone to a better working life.

Another co-worker, June, meanwhile, spent much of a recent day cleaning the lobby, a job seemingly conceived as a pain in the ass (and in the lower back, shoulders and, of course, neck).

One of our several supervisors, John, shows the empathy of a cocklebur, and his criticism sends June, who has been dealing with her mother's serious illness, to the locker room in tears.

John is something of a perfectionist, which is fine. Military background, I'd say. By the book. Here's how you do this. No frills or flowers. Showed me just today how to change the ketchup pouch in the stainless-steel dispenser with its soft plastic guts and hard plastic throat, and if he started by saying, "No, not *that way*!" well, so what? I needed the help.

He came in about mid-afternoon today, though, and missed several hours of a surprise rush, visitors driven indoors by heavy squalls of snow. Cashiers, also handling drinks (including countless cups of cappuccino and hot chocolate) were besieged; runners slapping ordered foods on brown plastic trays were bedraggled; cooks bent over hot grills and ovens were scrambling and sweating.

They all, at least, worked in company. June handled the lobby alone. Cleaning tables. Sweeping floors. Bagging trash. Replenishing cup lids and stir sticks, onions and peppers, mayonnaise and mustard, sugar-and-seasoning bins and comment cards. Mopping spills. Wiping up dreck. When the crowd receded, I stepped out to help.

Honestly? I hate that lobby job, and I don't see any of the managers (besides John) hurrying out to do it, either. A cashier can at least find variety in the changing array of faces and clothing and attitudes, in answering questions and trading observations. Runners and cooks can joust with jokes or talk a little baseball or park politics amid the gastronomic waves. And these other echelons can take some pride in performing, in applying their minds to recording and assembling the orders, handling the cash, dispensing the food.

The lobby person scours the bottom of the fast-food barrel. The lobbyists pick up unwanted remains, clean what others dirty, provide what others take for granted. And if they work nimbly and well, their performance reflects more upon the institution and its management than upon themselves. They are ghosts in the machine.

A supervisor, though, is no ghost. John lit into June, who cried, and I like to think that was the beginning of the end for him.

Now, among visitors and refugees in the Lodge near 8PM, I can look west again to Old Faithful, with the wind carrying the vapors directly away from us, and I see its newest steam roiling up a hard dark gray against the dispersing and brightly sunlit mists that preceded it. The effect is striking, and novel. This is not a one-trick pony.

The night before, walking back to the dorm, I had stopped in slanting, wind-borne snow to regard the geyser in complete solitude. The pathways, each introduced by a familiar wooden Old Faithful sign, penetrate from the outer rim to the inner like spokes in a wheel, with pines filling the gaps, and at that moment one of the lodgepoles issues loud creaks, a wonderfully non-human commentary. I have also seen one of the rangers, narrating with skill and panache to a captive crowd in front of the Visitor Center, likening the earthen crust over the Yellowstone caldera to the crust over a pie, and the geysers and pools and fumaroles to holes a mother (in his words) would poke in it with a fork, so it wouldn't explode.

I can take a lesson from it. Steam quietly. Erupt rarely. Never explode. But then, here in Wonderland, dreams of a better life and a better self can writhe within the tendrils of vapor, surely to be blasted by sunlight in the wider world. Keep moving forward, I figure, one step at a time.

Later in the week, snow floats in again, shifts to hard-driven pellets, regresses to soft flakes, gives way to bursts of sun through pillars of cumulus. On my way to Grant Village through these snowy curtains in the Buick to work an elliptical training machine, I listen to Dvorak's "New World Symphony" and its haunting, hymn-like refrain, and I think of a brief conversation I had with Veronika of Slovakia, whom I haven't seen in three or four days, about another Czech (or Slovak) composer, Smetana, and his musical rendering of the tumbling River Moldau. We wonder what he would make of Yellowstone's myriad of waterways, from the Lamar River's slow meanders to tumbling freshets feeding the rippling Firehole and the raging Yellowstone and Gallatin. She might say (lacking her company, I have to make up her side) that he wouldn't know of them, and I could come back with the latest news flash from National Public Radio, which (oddly) plays in the public restrooms in the little Snow Lodge vestibule linking the Geyser Grill with a neighboring Gift Shop. The announcer, anticipating a Dvorak work, points out that the composer spent many years in the United States and borrowed themes from folk tunes and native American music.

As I write this, Veronika, in her plum-colored dining room attendant's uniform, taps me on the shoulder (!), and I tell her about that musical discovery (she didn't know). She tells me how tired she is from lifting trays of dirty dishes while continually smiling (she did this in a dance troupe back home, she says) and that she has to work through Saturday without a day off. I wish I could offer other options, but I can't. In her weariness and the flush of work she looks prettier than I remember. I have been alone for almost 10 years; glad to have a few hormones left, but please, geez, get real.

9
LONER AT
LONE STAR

No more easy breeze on the boardwalk. Time for the climb to Lone Star.

In the Old Faithful Visitor Center, I have told a ranger (as hikers here are encouraged to do) that I am going running this afternoon on the trail to Lone Star Geyser. Don't go alone, she advises. And don't run.

For lack of a partner (preferably a cute and bright and lively woman) with a similar pace, and out of a determination to keep running until I can't anymore, I disobey on both counts. The ranger says, "Grizzlies don't like to be surprised. And they sometimes go after anything running."

Oh, and have a nice time.

I riff through a few bear stories: the day-hiker who surprised a female grizzly and her cubs near Lake Village and took four bloody furrows down his back, the overnighter shredded near his campsite on White Lake by a bear attracted to his foodstuffs, the photographer who missed his last closeup of eyes, nose and teeth. Never mind that many more visitors to Yellowstone die from drowning or scalding or suicide.

That day, not wanting to vanguard the victims list in 2005, I wimp out, instead reprising the main boardwalk and adjoining trail from Old Faithful to Biscuit Basin. I warn clusters of camera-toters with "on your left!" miss a Grand Geyser eruption by minutes, and pass two of my favorite and at that moment placid geysers: Solitary and Spiteful.

That's often described me, lately. I might not appear that way, sitting at this same table night after night in Old Faithful Lodge with my laptop, surrounded by diners, watching Old Faithful through the wavy glass. But I don't have much to say to these people, or to the fellow workers I sit near in the EDR (Employee Dining Room).

Desperate for work, repeatedly turned down, increasingly avoiding society, muttering with impatience at drivers who crawl or race or move without signaling and even at my 82-year-old mother, who for the better part of the last two years has given up most of her modest comforts to feed me, I can be a pain in my own butt. Running releases me from self-judgment and all swarming daily concerns.

I don't want to share anyone else's. The foot traffic on these fumarole-dodging paths may have arrived in enormous vans and SUVs, but at the moment they spew reactions, witticisms, wonderments and inanities, not carbon monoxide or engine noise.

Looping back at the basin near a piping pool, I come up on a tattooed, woolen-capped, much-pierced group of young Goths as one of them, wired to satellite radio, announces, "Dude, I just heard (a rock musician, name unclear) shot himself!" The unfortunate dude, a celebrity in another dimension, is as unknown to me as the asshole who threw the first beer can into Morning Glory Pool.

Two days later, under a bright blue sky, my time has come. No more wimping.

I step back into Old Faithful's main ranger station, and I encounter a nurse named Jennie from the adjoining clinic who says she runs and notes that part of the Lone Star trail still shows snow that discourages bears and should be safe. She adds, "If you're alone, you might think about bear (pepper) spray. They sell that up at the General Store." I can imagine Goth Boy later the same day, spouting "Dude, I just heard some guy up on Lone Star today peppered himself and got eaten by a bear!"

At its height, the Lone Star Trail debouches from a modest marker at the end of a parking lot just south of the Kepler Cascades and snakes down past Bitterroot. I'm on the uplift. As I start on the pine-shaded stretch of asphalt and cinders, a ballad from a Disney TV series when I was a kid in the '50s dances into my head: "Kilt him a bar...when he was only three. Dayyy-VEEE, Dayyy-vee CROCK-kett, king of the wild frontier!"

On this frontier, I am not king. I'm a skinny, idiot runner in eye-glasses and New Balance 603's and a shirt that reads "Winterfest 5K 2004," from Baraboo, and I expect that if a bear comes after me I will wet myself or worse and the person conducting the post-mortem will say, "Geez, what a wuss!"

The trail winds among deep stands of lodgepole beside the Firehole River and climbs to a rocky ridge, then skirts a meadow and bends through woodland and marsh to an open field, crowned with the 10-foot silicate cone and the outwash of Lone Star Geyser.

The climb through the early rocks siphons my fuel. Huffing, looking amidst the grasses for something van-sized, dark and furry, I wonder if, hearing a grizzly pound up behind me, I could seize a lodgepole sapling and deflect the attacker with parry and thrust. No. I would grab the young tree, give it a yank and sprain my scapular muscles, lower back and greater gluteus...after which I would probably prefer to be eaten.

Yellowstone's woods, regardless, are wilder than any I've run through. In America's increasingly developed lower 48 states, these belong to the Real Wild. Back in Wisconsin, the woodlands I knew at

Devil's Lake or Mirror Lake (except the parts open in hunting seasons) shelter deer and wild turkeys, mice and squirrels, foxes and a rare wolf or coyote and other raptors, including owls, hawks and eagles. But the fens and forest end quickly at highway or farm field or subdivision, and motor vehicles and hunters kill woodland creatures by the hundreds.

Out here, in forests stretching across thousands of acres, animals can stretch out, regain their instincts, lose their inhibitions. And the grizzly (if you don't count the federal government or the owner of the biggest surrounding ranch) is king.

No carnivores today. The woods are sheltering, the meadows welcoming, the cone of Lone Star Geyser quiet. I am not "kilt by a bar."

I get back through mostly downhill to a shower, and I report to work. One of the other guys doesn't show up, and I get extra duty. After five or six hours, Ron-slash-Ole says, "You're walking like your feet hurt."

My feet are fine. The rest of me needs rehab.

10
WILDLIFE IN
THE MIDST

Winter is still with us. On this snowy first of June, logs burn behind the iron grate of a large stone fireplace at the north end of the Old Faithful Lodge. How many of the humans who wander near for warmth realize that they are stepping near an animal's doorway?

I'm bent over the laptop, often looking up. Words, even with me as the drover, can be boring, especially when ill-used. I'm struggling, so I scan the room.

Two seats to my right, on the maroon-and-beige carpet under another of the dining room's wood-and-wicker chairs, a small chipmunk holds a potato chip to its mouth and chitters through it. He has been bolting-and-freezing-and-bolting around the room's north end, near the fireplace, even making a run at the tables of a few startled or bemused patrons. I wonder at the staff's inattention. Maybe if somebody screams... Then the rodent (pygmy squirrel sounds better) makes a seemingly feckless dash at where the stone fireplace meets its apron and plunges into a billfold-sized crevice.

After the tables empty, I imagine the chipmunk darting ahead of the industrial vacuum on the night's last cleanup, snagging scraps. Then I think of the mouse in Disney's "Ben and Me," and of E. B. White's storied Stuart Little and his human family, and I wonder if the chipmunk is listed among the staff as "night cleanup."

He should be. As the evenings of May pass into June, I see him every night. He's allowing me to share his space, or he's maybe too hungry to care. I wonder if he has other mouths to feed.

A few minutes later, a ruddy-faced, pudgy little boy chases the chipmunk into its hole, bends over the opening and growls. I would like to see him do that with a grizzly. I really would. What possesses him? Maybe he's descended from some of the buffalo-hunters who slaughtered bison for trophies and sport, leaving the carcasses to rot across the Great Plains. Maybe he's just another hyper-active, violence-mimicking child of today. Play-acting is fine, to a point. But don't threaten an animal. Where are the parents?

I resist intervention. Still, I'm rooting for the chipmunk.

Over my shoulder, I hear Veronika gently training a new recruit named Luka in the art of bussing tables in the O.F. Lodge cafeteria. Try not to clean up too close to people eating, she says. The noise can bother them. Good advice. "Thank you very much for your help," she says. Good add-on.

Today was pretty slow, she says, in the afternoon when I am back with her in the unpredictable ebb-and-flow of food service. "One evening I was here completely alone," she is saying, "and everything was *full*. I had 300 people asking me the same thing: give me a clean table." She kept smiling. She did her best. She then talks of a polka festival in a small village in the Czech Republic (Luka is Czech), from her dancing days. I hear the spritz-spritz-spritz of the cleaning bottle, the squeak of the cloth on Formica. "We had a lot of fun," she says. Then, coming up from behind, she gestures to me and says, "This is our colleague." I stand and shake Luka's rubber-gloved hand, and he smiles shyly.

Coming back to the bunk, well past dark, I encounter another mammal, much bigger. The lights on poles overhead are strung out in pools along the path, leaving shadows, the largest a long shadow alongside the dorm. I look a little left as I approach the front door, and I see something glitter. An eye.

From the dark, an enormous profile takes shape. He's lying there, alone, looking at me from under a dark curly mane and horns held high.

Bull bison.

I stop a few feet away, and we look at each other. I say "hell-ooo," in my most soothing tone. He lowers his head, just a little. I can't help feeling that this guy is closer to me than anyone else here. "Good night," I say. He stays in shadow. The door closes behind me.

It almost penetrates my numbness to wake up on June 9th to that particular silvery daylight reflected off snow. More winter? *Really?* I look out over the Bitterroot parking strip to a dreamscape of snow-flocked pines climbing in legion into the serpentine of hills, and below the crowns are myriad bright green saplings, their snow coats giving the area the look of a children's Christmas fantasy. Snow slides in rectangles off the corrugated metal roofs of the dorm and pub and nearby service buildings and lands in muffled "plumpfs." As I walk to breakfast, I pass the marshes where three elk graze on exposed green grasses. Beyond them, a bison pendulates toward the Old Faithful Inn. These neighbors I like! Might as well let the solitary bull book a berth in Bitterroot, nice cozy stall out back. I could join him. I'd take straw over our mattresses any time.

11
LIFE AS WE KNOW IT

Shortly after 8PM on Friday, June 3, Old Faithful produces an especially good show. "There it GOES!" "Oooooooh!" "Oohhhhhh!" In the view from inside the Lodge, the strongest jets surpass the tops of the high windows. As it begins its fallback, a father speaks in the voice adults sometimes use with small children. "Now it's YOUR size. Pretty cool, huh? It's STILL going. Look at it!" Moments later, he says, "Still going!" I pitch a small part of my blueberry muffin at the crack in the fireplace; to my amazement, just as it lands the chipmunk begins to emerge, and the morsel hits the little guy on the head! He quickly sinks back, and I hope I haven't scarred him for life.

What's this? Now small patchy-gray mouse appears, about the color of the fireplace stone, not the chipmunk at all, and pulls the large morsel down onto a little stone shelf, unseen before, where I can see his head move and a small black eye as he eats. Have I discovered a polyglot community of rodents, sharing the dining room spoils?

If so, they are an improvement over the human lot sharing Bitter-root dorm. The kid next door, from Alabama, seems agreeable enough. Sandy, tow-headed look. Easy grin. But early on I find the acrid odor of cigarette smoke—a rarity now in shared spaces—in the bathroom and begin to understand why he keeps leaving on the exhaust fan.

Then I find a stubbed-out, filtered butt in the toilet. One night, past midnight, the snapped-on light illuminates the bathroom doorframe, and he and a girl talk loudly about how many states they've been to and what they saw there, keeping me awake another half hour. Then, just today, as I have just come back from a run to Lone Star and waited to shower, he and a male friend start bantering. "I got my stuff stashed out in the woods, so I can go grab it," one voice says, and the other says, "Fifty bucks an ounce. Shit!" Then the first voice says, "That kid at Wendy's looked like he was a junior or senior in high school. I thought, great, we got fuckin' Romper Room here! But that stuff he had…"

"Was good shit, man," his cohort concludes.

I have discovered the Yellowstone counterculture. Reefer madness at work! Should I narc him out? Probably. I should at least mention the smoking to someone in authority, but the bearded and long-haired residence supervisor looks more like a pothead than my neighbor back in Bitterroot, who's always wheeling his mountain bike around out front or playing hacky-sack. Not that I'm judging him on such scant evidence. I decide to let the weed burn through.

My first question is how the hell this kid knows about Romper Room. I used to watch it in the '50s, along with Ding Dong School and Miss Frances. Is the retro media machine so thoroughly engaged that nothing is safe in its context or time anymore?

I'm glad, at least, to find a few older souls among the herd of young bucks. In the hall in the dorm one day, I encounter a guy two rooms down, pushing out through his door. He sticks out his hand but does not smile. His name is Mel. I call him Mel of the Woeful Countenance. He is also the first African-American I have seen here, and his face shows lines of weathered ebony. I hear him in the hall, a few days later, in this exchange:

"Have a good one, Mel."

"I won't. But you have one, though."

For me, the day is not good. My fifth consecutive day's work ends in a dramatic few moments down in the locker-slash-counting room. Ron (cum Ole), the majordomo, has just riffled through my day's "cash drop," something more than $1,200 according to the register tape (the total, with credit cards, edges just under $2,000), and I see his back and neck stiffen.

"Something's wrong here," he says. "You're off 60 dollars and 42 cents."

"Under?"

"Under."

Sixty bucks short. Men have been kicked onto the open road with their possessions in a handkerchief for less. Men have been kicked IN their open road first.

I handle the money all day. Some of the bills are a little wet, a little greasy. Some of them are germ-ridden, no doubt. Fresh imports from the Far East, where the avian flu looms, or from Africa, with its tuberculosis, or from suburbs, where people pretend they're safe. "Wash your hands as often as you can," the bosses say, but they don't enforce that. Try stopping for a wash during a rush.

As it was, that day's rush was in full swing when I showed up at 11:15AM, and it lasted three and a half hours. There was a 10-minute lull. I had time to drop crayons and Tootsie pops into the deck of kiddie meal bags. Then the rush kicked back in for another hour and a half, an incessant, unrelenting parade of faces, in singles, twos, threes, sixes, swam toward the counter, repeating varying combinations of the menu, "We'll take..." "We need..." "I'll have..." "Give me..." and, occasionally, asking for ingredients ("Is your chicken fried in anything with peanut oil?" "Are there any dairy products in your soup base?" No, I could say, but there's enough cholesterol to take 10 years off your miserable life) and, sometimes, changing their minds after the order has been processed, forcing me to call for the manager (because the computer program won't let me back in).

I see Mel again a few days later and learn that he had worked the graveyard shift twice this week. Couldn't sleep in daylight. Dog tired. He talks of a month or two from now, moving to San Diego or San Francisco, finding work. I wish him good luck, and I mean it.

The next morning, I hear from the hallway, "Get up, Richie. You can sleep when you're dead." I think of Mel, and I want to tell him that as long as we are dog-tired and footsore, we know that we're still among the living.

12
DAY OF WONDERS

A short Sunday (10AM to 3PM) at the GUG (Geyser Under Ground) allows an afternoon run, and from the time I stop in at the clinic (to be told that Ranger Jennie, the runner, isn't there but works Mondays through Thursdays) and take off toward the boardwalk of the Upper Geyser Basin in a gratifying surge, the day produces magic.

First, as I swing north past the lodge, up the hill over the Firehole River and toward the Lion group, Beehive erupts just below me. I hustle over. The geyser's modest bump is well-named. Its spurt is thin and powerful, as if from a fire hose; a fellow onlooker informs me that the nozzle-like opening is just four inches across (we are full of these factoids, now, aren't we? Of course, I should check; trust and verify. But I don't need calipers to enjoy the display).

Then, as I pound past the turnoff to Castle, I notice a sudden surge from its battlements and turn quickly toward it. In my several visits, and in the month here, I have never seen it perform. Now I do, and the wait is worth it.

Castle produces a series of jets that reach 100 feet or more, and, like the choreography of a great fireworks display, it surges, ebbs, surges again in fresh columns. It goes five minutes, 10 minutes. Steaming water spills in torrents down its walls and across its base, running mostly south to the river. It goes on so long that I can feel my calves stiffen and have to leave, continuing north to Biscuit Basin.

Grotto geyser, though not in full play, is active enough to fog my glasses as I pass. The path up and over the hill near Daisy is muddy from the day's rains, the footprints of visitors have filled with reddish water, turning the area a kind of inverted appaloosa, and I can feel the slop on my legs. (Visitors in snow clothes seem surprised to see me in shorts, but running turns up the heat).

After I circle the basin and regain the boardwalk, I see, firing away in front of me, Riverside! I watch it for several minutes, arrayed against a piney backdrop, spraying the Firehole in silicate panache. I have hit the thermal trifecta. Riverside, too, outlasts me, and I head past a dozing Grand Geyser feeling good, though I try to ignore my inner checklist and the tremor of a nerve in my left leg.

Then, at dinner in the EDR, Roger, the good spirit from Taiwan who won the company free-throw contest by hitting 12 of 15, tells me he is leaving that night to go home (bus to Bozeman, plane to Denver, another plane to L.A., another plane—did he say a nine-hour flight?—across the Pacific) and says come sit at our table and would you sign my book?

The pretty young Thai woman next to him, who is wearing a pink sweater, pulls out a chair for me. I write something inane in his book, such as "To a fine basketball player and a good guy, best wishes, blah blah." I manage to spill salad on the pink sweater; I apologize, and the woman laughs and squeezes my arm. As I read my Wallace Stegner book on the Mormon migration (*The Gathering of Zion: The Story of the Mormon Trail*), five of the workers from Taiwan and Thailand talk in a melodious skitter and laugh and gesture with great animation. As surely as anyone, they are migrating, too.

As he leaves, Roger turns to me and says, "Hope to see you again" and "God bless you," and I smile my best and say, "Same to you." The particular god doesn't matter. Whichever we share, I know we won't see each other again.

Then, trailing a sudden shower, the northeastern horizon fills with a vivid, enormous rainbow, its colors vibrant from the overarching red to the underpinning purple. Vehicles rashly pull over, drivers leap out with cameras: a polychrome block!

As I'm bent to the laptop in the Lodge's dining room, Veronika stops to say hello and talks of a noon rush that filled every table (there must be nearly 200) with only her and one other worker to keep them clean and available. (At the grill we suffered that same noon rush, two hours full tilt with three cashiers).

Veronika was, she says, literally plowing a path before each new group to get a table ready, showing her florescent smile and balancing dishes. I can watch her, now, moving gracefully with an easy sway, carrying a stack of plates, her smile visible from across the room. Her greatest wish in the press of humanity, she says, was for a drink of water. But she didn't have time.

To end the evening, one more triumph: my friend the chipmunk reappears from his lodging in the fireplace and dashes past my feet. I hear him nibbling something a few feet away. New experiences; old friends. A good day!

13
GRAND PLANS

June fattens toward July, and I'm feeling a little beaten down, not in the running but in the daily grind. I bump into those nagging gremlins of, "How did I end up here?" and, "What's wrong with me?" Didn't I used to be a writer?

I am already on the brink of dissolution one fine day in the Grill when Mr. Potato Salad steps up. He is Japanese and has, I quickly realize, almost no English. He leans his head almost sideways and says, "Potato salad?" No, I'm sorry, I tell him. No potato salad. A crowd is building behind him. This is the third hour of a three-hour rush. Voices rise. Heat half-smothers us. He narrows his eyes and says, more assertively, "Potato salad!" No, no, sorry, I say. We have potatoes—the French fry—and we have salad, the tossed and the chicken. No potato salad. He stares. One of his companions orders a cheeseburger. We have those. Another orders the kiddie meal, with the nuggets. Here's your bag and kiddie cup. We turn back to customer number one. He looks pained. "Potato salad?" he says.

When in doubt, pass the buck. "They might have some in the cafeteria, at the Lodge," I say. If he continues, I COULD send him to the EDR, where potato salad is a staple.

"Potato," the man says. "Salad."

I lock into the idea of flexible customer service. I imagine myself saying, "Sure, sir, we can do that for you," and I am taking the French fries and shoving them into the tossed salad. I am slapping on a dollop of mayonnaise. I am stirring vigorously. I am stepping around the counter, wearing a cheesy smile, and I am extending the little plastic tub. He is staring at it, uncertainly, and taking a step back. I am plunging my hand into the mix, feeling the bottom of the plastic container rub against my knuckles, and I am lifting the sloppy product and smearing it into his hair, raking it down his face. And I say, "Potato salad!" Then I say, "Would you like that in the combo meal?"

Looking for a spark from the life-force, I kindle an idea for a story. Closed for nearly a year for maintenance and upgrades, the vaunted Old Faithful Inn will reopen later this month. I could delve into its history and challenges and write a piece for *The New York Times*. A natural! Might be my best chance to make the paper and keep my fingers in the printer's ink. I start asking around for old hands who know the sprawling complex best, and I hear about a long-time guide. When I find her, she talks a little about the inn's warm and historic spirit and points me to Yellowstone's archives, newly reinstalled in Gardiner. Perfect: I have a break from work right ahead!

Oops. The three days off that I'd seen on the schedule for next week have been cut to just two. Hello, Blue Monday. This has something to do with our co-worker June quitting, or threatening to, or with Jake leaving; as the angel in "It's a Wonderful Life" told Mr. Stewart's Harry Bailey, "Every life touches so many other lives." Can I dig up enough background and foreground to narrate the Inn's reopening?

Concerning that structure, Ron/Ole says at work, "We'll be losing two more people when the Inn opens." Oh, good. Maybe I'll have seven days a week of all-day rushes to cherish. Six bucks a fucking hour, and I'll be fried by mid-July.

I hear Dad saying, again, as he does whenever I ask about how his third wife Ellen is doing and picture him taking care of her as he's getting shit for it, "We take it one day at a time."

I've read what I can in the most venerated book of Yellowstone history, volume one of Aubrey L. Haines's *Yellowstone Story*, so the first day-off sends me to Gardiner.

The new Yellowstone National Park Heritage and Research Center is a palace of Postmodern polished stone, brass fittings, airy spaces, pastel-cowled lights, minimal ornament. Launching my research on the Old Faithful Inn, I try to feel comfortable there, but I don't. What repels me might be the preternatural cleanliness and the odor of scholarship.

Please understand: the world depends upon good, honest scholars. I'm not bad-mouthing them, although if you want to talk about shoddy, or half-assed, or utterly unimportant scholarship, well, I could refer you to the fine man mentioned above, Dr. Drummond Rennie, former Deputy Editor of the *New England Journal of Medicine* and an authority in high-altitude medicine.

He came by his knowledge the hard way, rescuing climbers on the highest mountains. He also learned a hard lesson about scholarship. Dr. Rennie once told me (and an audience in Omaha) that fully half of the studies received by the *New England Journal*, studies already approved, mind you, by peer reviewers, are shoddily done or fatally flawed. All-too-many media creatures, especially in TV and on the web, report conclusions of studies from a press release or an E-blast. As Dr. Rennie advised, I don't trust reports or conclusions of *any* study until I see the details on how it was carried out.

I *do* understand the squeeze applied to most of these researchers, especially the poor schlemiels teaching a full load and supporting a family who would rather TEACH well than humbug around putting together fodder for scholarly journals that hardly anyone will read.

As a humble former writer of feature stories for newspapers I can't aspire even to that, but maybe I can still manage a tiptoe into the big time with a piece on a popular place.

The archive gives me a pamphlet from the Inn's original opening, June 1, 1904, and a host of maps, drawings and photos to run through the Xerox, showing the grace and beauty of Robert Reamer's original sloped-roof, dormer-studded log structure in the years before boxy three-story wings for tourists (and profits) were shot-gunned on.

You should see the vast log lobby, climbing a peaked roof to 76 feet, and its surrounding multi-level balconies and enormous fireplace. Still there! A room in the original building has kept its character, as I learned in a visit. Rooms in the wings…don't ask. No amenities, bad heating and cooling, sad décor.

But the Inn itself has kept its charms. If I can slip in for a gander and a walk through the empty Bear Pit Lounge, a symphony of carved glass, I'll have enough to start a story.

Hying back to Old Faithful, I take my car to the YSS (Yellowstone Service Station), boxed oil filter in hand, for an oil change. While someone named Paul is schlepping the oil, the jovial proprietor (truth is, I can rarely tell in this Disneyland of Hospitality whether someone is *really* jovial or just good at projecting it) tells me a sobering story about elk.

He opens by extolling the care that bison, cows and bulls alike, bestow on their light tan, unhumped, incredibly cute calves. "Wolves and grizzlies don't usually mess with the calves," he says. "Bison defend their young. And I mean they'll COME AFTER anything that threatens a calf. Have you seen how fast bison can be? And, man, they are BIG."

He adds the tale of a visiting truck driver who became impatient in a bison block and moved too close to a bull. That bull let him pull alongside and then pounded and raked the cab with his head and horns, causing a few thousand bucks in damage and a dramatic attitude reassessment by the driver. The service station manager concludes, "A lot more people are hurt by bison every year than by bears." I am now a sworn member and supporter of Team Bison.

Elk, on the other hand, he says, seem to prefer self-preservation and abandon their helpless young to oncoming carnivores. "I saw a lot of elk calves in April and May," he said. "I hardly see any now."

I am not consoled by the thought that the Yellowstone elk count seems stable, even with the reintroduction of wolves and flourishing of bears. I want to get out there and defend those little four-hoofed guys. If I do, who will defend me?

14
HAPPY TO SEE YOU!

The two-footed dorm guys are dramatists. One of them, in the hall, shouts, "Hey! Ain't nobody gonna come by and say hi to me?" Answer: won't say hi, won't say boo. He's not angling for my answer, of course. He's angling for a little attention from the frowsy babe in the half-open blouse.

The same voice erupts later that night, after, apparently, someone has knocked on his door. "I don't wanna hear another fucking knock on my fucking door," he says. "You knock on my fucking door again, we're gonna have a PROBLEM!"

The next morning, which is gentle and sunny, I find Mel sitting on the front concrete stoop, finishing a cigarette, and I ask if the voice in question kept him awake. "Naw," he says. "I was too worn out from work. And I had a little something to drink, so nothing was gonna wake me up." I offer what I imagined I'd say to the voice in question, "If this is the way you solve problems, then the only question is which prison system you end up in," and Mel says, "A couple of these guys WERE in prison. They didn't used to hire people with a record, but they are, now." Comforting. Hey, guys, anybody for Anger Management class? I hear they got some bitchin' broads there!

At work, I am managing anger pretty well, and then I am hit with a burst of sunlight.

I see, from the midst of another pressing crowd in the Geyser Grill, the faces of Dave Anderson (first seen in 1968, introduced as my room-mate in Ingersoll Hall at Colorado State), and his wife Jennifer (I was best man at their wedding, in St. Mary's Church in Colorado Springs) and their first-born daughter Kajsa (whose birth I experienced from just outside a hospital door and who had just earned her dental degree) and older son Davin (the bright-eyed little guy who became the top-ranked triathlete in NCAA Division I at Colorado) and younger son Danyon (a high-energy ray of sunshine determined to become a physician) and Kajsa's husband, Dan Novembre (who races dirt bikes and something between a go-cart and a tank up and down mountains) and a pretty young woman I don't recognize. She turns out to be Trish, the woman Davin has just proposed to in an elaborate scheme involving a bag with tent pegs that actually held a ring.

They have found me. They invite me to dinner in the Snow Lodge, at the best place, and when I finish my shift and count the money (about ten bucks to the good), I go. The day has been crazy, with at least a four-hour rush and the woman on the next register (a newbie) poking me in the shoulder now and then to ask basic questions while I am trying to process the barrage of orders and keep the cooler stocked and assisting in the lobby and…you know the drill. At times the new-comer appears florid and overwrought, and even the new lobby woman from Czechoslovakia, so hard-working and capable, grabs my arm and says, "Help me!" And I try but can't because the mass of customers is surging toward my register. So, the adrenaline is pumping.

I am very glad to see Dave and his family, feeling slightly proud and a little awkward in the Yellowstone cap and shirt (worrying that my miseries might emerge). Hugs. Prime rib. The story of Davin's discovery that he loves his beautiful and athletic fiancée, and of her love for him, and talk about knowing love and its importance and its awful imitators, and a waitress hovering near who recognizes me and treats me in a friendly way, and I am talking so much about Chris and Lynn and the following marital disaster with Kathy that I am slow with the salad and even slower with the prime rib and apple pie. In the dinner derby, I am dead last (as I always was with the Anderson family in their house on Hill Street in Colorado Springs. With nine kids, you learn to pounce).

These are incredibly good people. I feel a little sad and awkward in my current misery, but I talk about it anyway and feel better for it. Dave nearly always has an apt and positive response, and Jennifer is among the best listeners and best mothers in my experience. They indulge me.

We resolve to meet the following morning, a Sunday (July 3) and my day off. They take me and Davin and Trish, the real newcomer to Yellowstone, and Danyon, to whom every outdoor experience is a novelty to be celebrated, on a liberating walk, down an old freight road toward the Ojo Caliente hot spring and then, magically, on a sharp left toward the unknown.

The "trail," a dirt swath of vague margins through clumps of juniper and sage and buffalo chips, bends and elevates to a bald white space that's obviously a "thermal feature." I'm thinking pool, but when we come near, we hear the guttural moan of steam whistling through a rocky throat and then the irregular plopping of bubbling mud.

This is only the preface. Welcome to Pocket Basin, a place not noted on official maps.

Beyond and to the east we find whole encampments of holes filled to varying degree with stewing, gurgling, heaving and pitching white mud, here simmering and fizzing with tiny bubbles, there offering enormous bubble domes, over there catapulting thick droplets that sometimes hit our shoes and shins. As Dave notes, each mud pot is different; while most of the mud is bright white, some is beige, some brown, and its thickness varies from watery to rubbery. Some mud pots are bone dry.

The two most liberating parts of the experience involve orientation and perspective, ours and Dave's. We have left the boardwalks, left the road, left the human confinement of regulation and fenestration.

Orientation: We are hiking overland and discovering sights as astounding as any that have been labeled and plotted for convenient observation by park planners, and we are entirely on our own. *We* decide how close we can step over the thermal crust to the varying displays. *We* pick the path through the bleached fallen and uprooted tree trunks. *We* stumble across discoveries that I can only call magical.

The ending is a dramatic set of pots that offer both the vigorous fizz and the slow expanding burst. As we climb the next ridge and overlook a reed-collared lake, rarely seen by tourists, Danyon pees on a pot-holed rock and then carries it up as a souvenir worth his father's 50 cent bounty. His father gently puts it back.

Perspective: Dave proves his statement that the greatest wonders of Yellowstone show not in the grandiose sights, showy as they are, but in the detail. He stops to consider elements of the landscape unlisted on any map or guide. The first moves over calmer water nearest the shore of the Firehole: he tries to comprehend the design. Maybe this is a small metaphor for life. They move almost in loops, flying 10 or 20 feet up, cutting back five or 10 feet, flying out again, but in patterns that elude our eyes. We want to know how, and why. We can only begin to guess. But this reinforces Dave's main point about the greatest (or at least the most complimentary) wonders of Yellowstone showing in the details.

Our lunch, at a block of three picnic tables beside the flurrying Firehole River, consists of peanut butter and banana sandwiches, Grannie Smith apples and white chocolate chip cookies baked by Davin. Why do I think the food tastes better outdoors? Maybe it's the fresh air. More likely, just now, it's the company.

15
RUSHED

The Geyser Grill is home not only to Wheat Montana bagels and Old Faithful Ale and buffalo burgers (taken, we were assured, from commercial herds in South Dakota and not from our bison homies) but also to a provocative pandemonium:

The Geyser Rush.

Newcomers to the staff learn very quickly in peak season to watch for the latest outburst of Old Faithful as it crowns above the trees, especially around breakfast or lunchtime. As soon as the plumes start to drop, the clustered crowd starts to leave.

Most of the multitude seems to stampede for the Geyser Grill. I've seen more than 200 people crowd into the service area, forming lines and leaning forward. One day a fire around the grill cut the power and filled the place with smoke. A handful of customers departed; the rest wanted food, and ours was still warm. That left us to take orders by hand. Some of my younger co-workers had never done a manual backup and had no clue about pads and pencils, much less adding columns of figures in their heads. I found pencil-work easier than navigating four order screens and their legions of colorful rectangles.

For the uniformed minions of the Geyser Grill, and for beleaguered workers and supervisors in shops and eateries throughout the park, the tourist supernova (I've been told) flares on the weekend of July 4th. Yellowstone attracts some four million visitors a year, and the majority seems to swarm around that red-white-and-blue banner of mid-summer. I'd rather face the bears and bison and wolves...prudently, I mean.

The hungry hordes *are* descending in earnest, and July tightens my focus and wears me out. I do have a day, one day amidst the tumult, when I log the highest receipt total of the summer on a single register. Any success is welcome. Most days I'm scrambling and sometimes feel overwhelmed.

Regardless, my greatest relief from compressed crowds and numbing routine comes in my runs on the back trails: the Howard Eaton Trail to Lone Star Geyser and Kepler Cascades, the Fairy Creek Trail to Fairy Falls and Imperial Geyser, trails to Mystic Falls and Mallard Lake.

Some tumbles of Howard Eaton are tough, especially a span of uphill through and over rocks, but the woodlands (as always) feel welcoming, and I love the stretches along creeks and through marshes and across open meadows, even if bears or wolves are known to appear there.

The Fairy Creek Trail is a mostly flat godsend, especially on a hot day. It starts from a parking lot just south of the great technicolor spring known as Grand Prismatic, simmering and shimmering, painting the air above with vapors of yellow, orange, red, green and blue: an aerial prism, scattering light in a rainbow. It's advertised as America's largest hot spring and third largest in the world (behind Boiling Lake in Dominica and Frying Pan Lake in New Zealand), and tourists flock over a curving boardwalk.

The trail keeps its distance, curling away into a grassland studded with small pines and then into deeper woods, playing tag with the small creek. On one unusually steamy day, I remember starting to wilt in the grasslands and to stagger through a series of curves and small rises, climbing a rise, then another, and then...

I could hear the whispering, first, then a murmuring, then a shushing, then a rushing. Up the last small hill, a clutch of rocks ahead, a sudden shadowing, I step through a magical curtain of cool air.

Fairy Falls, thin and wispy, drops 197 feet from the rhyolite rim of Madison Plateau and then glances off an intrusion of black magma and dives into hard rock below, where it has sculpted a grotto. I bask in the cooling spray, suddenly revived, and as I look up to the sunlit rim and then back to the grotto, I realize that this show goes on all the time, all seasons, all weathers, far more faithful than any geyser, far more rarely seen or felt. I wished, and still wish, that I could have bottled it and kept it with me.

From the grotto, the trail crosses Fairy Creek on a rough log bridge and then more or less follows the water to a meadow, busy with what the guides call "thermal features." A big hot spring, and a smaller one. A bubbling mud pot, and what looks like a placid pool. A wooden marker in the ground tells me otherwise: Imperial Geyser. I stand near the pool's edge for maybe 30 seconds, and blup, blup, BLAM, a jet of steaming water shoots into the air, falls back, shoots again, and again.

It isn't spectacular. So what? It's energetic and viewer-friendly, and I can stand as near or as far away as I like. Today I'm on a run, don't need to tempt broiling, so I start back. But I appreciate the freedom, the open invitation, the show for an audience of one. Just now, in this Imperial mood, I'm taking NO orders from anybody.

The next morning, I'm taking orders from everybody. Busy day. OK, man, happy face, happy voice, work the screens, work the keys, work the condiments, sweep the lobby, keep smiling! Most people are gracious, some even enthused.

Then, on a lobby sweep, I am kiltering my whipsaw physique through the dining area, brandishing my spray bottle of disinfectant, wipe rag fluttering from the off-hand, looking for tables to clean, condiments to stock, paper and plastic to replenish, when I come upon the table from hell.

I have been alone as the lobby swabbie for nearly three hours. Even with Bob there, as he was earlier today, I often feel alone, because Bob will ignore a dirty table right under his nose to tell a tableful of visitors some element of his life story (the stabbings—nine? fourteen? twenty-three?—and the poor childhood in Florida and the steel rod in the leg and the two heart attacks and the nearly 1,000 miles walking Yellowstone trails, often ending the conversation with, "Don't try to ride the buffalo!" I'm not doing him justice, because the man tells a good story). I have taken care of five booths—bing bing bing bing bing—and two small-squares when I turn and see…

Understand, most people are reasonably neat. A few leave a table so pristine that I can't tell it's been used, except that a salt-shaker might be slightly off-center.

This table, actually two of the smaller square ones pushed together, would have done Hieronymus Bosch proud. Ragged ribbons and chunks of animal flesh and vegetable matter, soiled fragments of napkin, battered cups, punctured plates and broken plasticware. If we had served eggs at that hour, I swear I would have found the yolks, smushed indelibly, and the whites, smeared all over, and the shells, ground into bits the size of glitter. The only clean areas are the erroneous zones where they covered the Naugahyde with their butts. I notice that, in one of them, someone's spilled drink has formed a heart-shaped pool. In cleanup terms, the triage challenge is staggering. This is not a nose job. This is a heart transplant. I have, oh, 45 seconds to a minute to suck it up and wipe it clean before another group gets up from its mess.

No whiners!

16
MUCH MORE
THAN WOEFUL

I happen upon Mel on the Bitterroot step, and we walk upstairs and start to talk about Mel's situation. He invites me into his room, notable for a large, glowing TV set and an intricate model sailing ship and several crystal liquor decanters lined up along the windows. He tells me more of his story. I know, already, that he's worked as a bellhop in at least two five-star hotels, one of them the Brown Palace in Denver, and he expands on that.

Coming out of the era of black porters on the Pullman cars, Mel learned his trade at resorts in the Poconos and Catskills, where he and a group of bellhops and porters, in some places entirely black, served a rich white clientele. They were abused at times, he says, and tells of a day when he and a co-worker added a laxative to a particularly odious white boss's coffee. Mel jumps up from the bed and, with something of a Charlie Chaplin walk and an agonized expression, demonstrates how the man leaped from his chair and shinnied toward the bathroom, soiling himself on the way.

Mel goes on to talk about tougher parts of his life, about being jumped in Boulder, Colorado. after coming from the bank, where he had cashed his paycheck, and being stabbed three times, a lung collapsed, his rent money gone, two months in a hospital bed. He talks about blowing thousands of dollars in casinos, and sometimes he says, "That was all my fault."

He lost his first wife, he says, after sleeping with her sister. "I was a hippie in those days, and stupid," he says. His first wife, he adds, is rich now. I can't recall his story about losing his second wife, except that it also involved fooling around.

Mel left his bellhop service in the Inn here two years ago, it turns out, after being arrested by rangers for DUI with a bunch of liquor in his car. "I was surprised they hired me back," he says, but he goes on to talk about knowing several guys here with felony records, who came directly to Bitterroot from halfway houses. "Some of them are cleaning hotel rooms," he says. "Can you believe that? In there with all the guests' stuff? And some are serving liquor. You don't want those guys serving liquor." He points to the next room, and I remember the threatening voice in the hall.

I had seen Mel, yesterday, in his purple uniform in the lobby of the Snow Lodge, briskly helping an older couple in with their luggage and blinking from his back-and-forths into the bright sunlight. He seemed to show just the right mix of dignity and subservience. His clients had their shoulders back and a look of satisfaction on their faces. If they walked any more stiffly, I reason, they might need some laxative with their coffee.

When he leaves Yellowstone, Mel says, he might go on out to San Diego, or try to start another business across the border. He has sold jewelry from a cart in a mall. For now, he's picking up a few bucks showing films to visitors and employees (he once made $400, he says,

renting a satellite TV setup to tourists for the Super Bowl). I can picture him as a younger man, good looking, engaging, playing jazz and
chasing women, and I feel a pang about how easy it is for a person
to wander off-course, just one bad decision, one impulsive move, one
wrong tack against the wind, and how hard it can be for him to get
back. Maybe one motive both for Mel and me to be here is to try to
reverse course…without having to face the loved ones we have hurt
and disappointed.

Pounding the trail from Bitterroot south toward Lone Star, I am
suddenly away from the madding crowd and its noisy-ass camper-vans,
trucks, buses, swarming sedans and sports cars, and gargantuan mobile
homes on wheels. I am running between cordons of lodgepole and
dandelions, escorted by pairs of pirouetting butterflies.

The initial climb hurts. I walk a fair amount. But on the level and
then back into the woods, the lungs start to come around, the legs
loosen. Atop the first big rise, looking back, I see the Old Faithful Inn
in full sprawl; atop the second I see the great ragged alabaster swash
of the Upper Geyser Basin; atop the third I see the distant snow-white
peaks of the Absaroka range.

The experience isn't transcendental. I'm in some pain, here, since
much of the climb is steep and stony. But the sense of remoteness in
those views feels good. The woods obliterate the torrent of traffic, the
gabble of voices, the pipings and rantings of boom boxes.

And on the way back, most of the run is downhill. Except for the
path's ruggedness and dodgy footing, I'd almost be airborne.

This is my prelude to work, which offers no inspiring views (except
darkening skies visible through the slats of the Geyser Grill's front
windows), no surprising turns and very little respite. The grill is hot,
today. Somebody reads the main room's thermometer and announces,
"89! (degrees F), and after the first four hours my left foot hurts and

my mouth feels as dry as the Sonoran Desert (I lived there two and half months last summer before being fired, so shut up and let me dramatize).

I fight off futility daily, fight off my inner useless-whining-wimp. But today's conditions bring me closer to that mewling complainer I dislike so much in myself. "A man is about as happy as he makes up his mind to be," Abraham Lincoln extols, via my father. So, on the Likert scale of happy-mind-make-up, today is a 3 or 4, a 10 being ecstatic, a zero being suicidal. I get the clear sense that I am working my way down.

At the finish, I visit the florid and bespectacled and basically sweet Erin in the Rec Center, to rent a movie about a computer-generated female. Erin is besieged by central Europeans who, with immigrant pioneer drive (or get-the-money-and-send-it-home imperative), are booking all the Internet time and renting all the movies. As I leave, I push past a couple of very hunky guys speaking Slovakian, and the woman I hear laughing and see looking up at them with that familiar (and yet somehow more animated than usual) smile, is Veronika. I pat her on the shoulder as I squeeze through. No-Chance Norris strikes (or is struck) again.

Just before that, as I am counting out the day's cash drop with Ole's supervision, he informs me that he may be moving on to Mammoth. "When they asked which (three) locations I wanted," he says, "I wrote Mammoth, Mammoth and Mammoth." A buddy of his, he says, would be co-supervisor. He has a line on a nice cabin down here, he says, with a bathroom. And if he gets it, he'll lobby to stay. If not... "Take me with you," I tell him. He laughs. "I'm serious," I tell him.

Then I ask for my paycheck for the last two weeks, and he provides it. The bottom line? Let's read the totals on the stub:

Hours: 51.6
Rate: $6.15
Amount: $317.34

Deductions:
EE MDC: $2.93
EE FIC: $12.56
WYROOM: $22.70
TETONT: $5.52
WYBORD: $91.95
Medcor: $8.40
NET PAY: $173.28

Room and board I get. What the hell is "TETONT?"

Let's see. I owe the WI SCTF, the child support people (and, through them, ex-wife Kathy and sons Alex and Ansel) $1,862. I owe the credit card folks $726.32 and Dell financing $200, for the laptop.

What am I, nuts?

Well, moving to Mammoth wouldn't change that. But I'd be a lot closer to Gardiner, and to opportunity. Another vagrant, misty dream.

At the bottom, the check adds a comment: "Make Yellowstone accident free!" I incline more toward a little cartoon on the window in the Snow Lodge counting room: "There are three kinds of people: those who can count and those who can't." I must be the third kind.

17
TRANSPORTED

I've never heard the phrase "downhill battle." On a warm day, in another hard slog up the Old Road, a few dizzy-stars dance in front of my eyes, and I find myself imagining (when my beleaguered brain allows) a better ascent. Something colorful and boisterous.

The Yellowstone Park Transportation Company, I've learned, started in 1886 as a stage line from the Northern Pacific railroad depot in Gardiner (designed by Robert Reamer) to the hotel in Mammoth. In those days, the Old Road was the ONLY road, and horses were the only propellant.

Welcome to the Tally-Ho stagecoach, rollicking and bumptious.

I picture Andy Devine or maybe Gabby Hayes or Fuzzy Knight up top, in bellicose narration. Yell all you want, but take it easy on those horses! From the Mammoth Hotel, visitors not shaken from their senses could climb onto Yellowstone Observation Wagons behind a four-horse team for park tours on the Grand Loop.

I try to imagine the trip back down to Gardiner, assuming the coach would mostly be empty and the horses much happier. Bet the butts and the shanks of all concerned still ached.

Motorcoaches came along within a decade or so, and then drivers worried about blown tires and bent axels and stall-outs. Not much romance in those, but by then a new paved highway snaked lower along the Gardner River and gave hoteliers, park guides and their customers faster and easier entry.

Long winters still confound access, but summer folk can see a line of snow coaches (trucks with heavy tires or belt-tracks) on company grounds in Gardiner, waiting to ferry visitors over snow-covered roads. They're faster and easier, too.

Faster and easier; how often does that phrase echo these days? The slower road promises more time to look and consider and imagine...

I'm on the rise now, on foot, no evidence of coaches in view, history behind me. One storm can erase most marks. And I don't tally, I tarry. But I can think of those days, now, as I push up the next hill, appreciating what this road offered in punishment and reward and what it meant for horses and drivers and to travelers. I'm glad (mostly) to be sharing that ground with memories of them.

I look at the crowded parking lots now with dismay. They are, for the most part, tucked away from the park's wonders, but the triumph of the auto and the suburban sprawl of the '40s, '50s and '60s spread their tentacles into Yellowstone. For me, the signature is a curving concrete ramp, the Old Faithful exit off the Grand Loop, which looks like a modernist's Interstate highway dream. Come you sedans, you station wagons, you Jeeps and Volkswagen busses and bugs, you SU-bleeping-Vs and massive Ford and Chevy and Dodge trucks, you haulers of campers and RVs, you pilots of fully-furnished escape vehicles the size of commercial buses. Yeah, I know, this is personal freedom. Capital F. Who needs to share a ride?

But we're missing the best rides. Good thing visitors can still find horses and saddle up. Or that they can at least dream about a gambol through rough country and leave Disneyland and Disney World where they belong. They could even try a two-legged ride on shoes for running and walking, up into the high country.

Get ready. I'm about to step to the heights.

18

UP THE PEAK

Call this Twin Peaks. Sorry, not David Lynch's quirky TV series of yore; this is the quirky series of days gushing into Yellowstone's prolonged summer rush.

The first peak is actual: Mount Washburn, 10,219 feet. I'll be climbing it with Melanie Moroney of the National Park Service, who has kindly invited me for the ascent. I had met Melanie (you might remember) in the NPS employment office in Mammoth, hoping for salvation, and maybe finding it.

She is benevolent and attractive and also married. I'm a little confused but glad to be with her.

This isn't a brave venture. We'll start somewhere near 7,000 feet on a forgiving footpath. But I'm curious to hear Melanie's thoughts, about her time in the park, about my job prospects with Jerry and Christina.

The second peak is psychological. We worker bees have been told that the Fourth of July can bring a sustained fusillade of tourists; get your ass ready to move.

The climb with Melanie is welcome. Just walking and talking together, I feel less alone. She's engaging and cautious. I'm standard-issue. Talking about Jerry adds energy to her voice and light to her eyes. Somewhere short of the top, we're greeted by mountain goats, maybe a dozen, bouncing over a ridge to the east. No chatter there, except of hooves. From the fire tower, we can see to Yellowstone Lake. "You'll like Jerry," she says.

Lost in the swarm of my own thoughts and concerns, I didn't appreciate Melanie enough, and I sidestepped a revelation. She was the first person there to see me not as an employee number or name on a weekly schedule or a dot-and-arrow on a workflow but as a *human being*.

I had come into the park from days riding equipment, cutting approaches and fairways and smoothing sand traps at Baraboo Country Club and riding a telephone and computer terminal in a booth among many at Lands' End, taking orders for clothes and sundries, following protocols. I existed as a job description, as a name on a schedule and timecard, just as I did in the Park.

The rescue started with people around me.

At breakfast the next morning in the EDR, I am joined by a guy named Brad, face fissured, hair long and scraggly, a product, I had thought, of late '60 and early '70s misadventures with drugs, or of some set of circumstances (divorce? bankruptcy?) that funneled him onto the streets.

"You know when I saw you out on the boardwalk the other morning?" he says. I nod. "Well, right after that, I heard someone calling 'Brad! Brad!', and I turned around and it was a woman I had known in Ogden. Never could find her down there, but here we are in Yellowstone, and there she is!"

I had thought of such an encounter only the night before, squeezing through a crowd in the lobby of the Lodge, wondering if at some point the many unfamiliar faces would suddenly reveal one I had known somewhere (Salt Lake? Akron? Fort Collins? Eugene? Exeter?). Nobody showed.

I ask Brad about Ogden, summoning vague memories of an Air Force Base and a downtown dominated by a couple of '20s brick buildings and grain elevators and a bend in I-15 and the Great Salt Lake's northern tip shimmering to the west, and by fresher memories of the Eccles Dinosaur Park (life-sized concrete and fiberglass renditions of the great beasts) with the boys two years ago, and a stop for cherries that didn't pan out (too early in the summer), and the regress south along the benches carved in the foothills by the old Lake Bonneville, past oil refineries and natural gas depots in North Salt Lake that my father had always pointed to, flame spouting from tall pipes.

Brad grew up there, he says; lived there nearly all his life. So, I tell him about my visit with Alex and Ansel to the dinosaur garden, and he talks about his father. "He killed himself when I was 5," Brad says. "He was an Ogden cop, got in a motorcycle accident that hurt his brain. He shot himself." Brad points an index finger at his own head and mimics the gunshot. "My brother and I saw him do it."

I wince, nod, say sorry, take a swallow of the Powerade/orange juice mix and press a thumb against the pages of *The Gathering of Zion*.

"Before he did it," Brad goes on, "he asked my grandparents to take care of the kids if anything happened to him," and Brad's mouth crimps and tears come to his eyes. "So they did," I say, and he nods.

"My brother ended up in prison," Brad says. "I took a different road. And now I'm here."

After he leaves with a "see ya," two young workers from Singapore sit down, and I wonder about their roads, but not enough to ask. I have trouble understanding their English, though, of course, it is infinitely better than my Chinese. We nod and smile and delve into our scrambled eggs.

19
LAST STRAW, NEW LOFT

Big changes in the wind. I find a welcome message from Melanie, the good-spirited and generous National Park Service personnel woman. Call Jerry Kahrs and Christina Jaffe-Kahrs at the Yellowstone Gallery in Gardiner about a job opening.

So, I do. Eight dollars an hour to start, and they might have an apartment for me in their basement. With a bathroom of my own. We can meet on my next trip up there, most likely this Thursday or Friday. It's a job interview, I know, and how many have I failed? But even the team once hauling the tourist stagecoach up the Old Road couldn't keep me away.

I like the thought of independence. Not sure the cash flow would be much better. More interesting products, though. And a way to get through the season, still visit Yellowstone, and have a place for visitors (couples, families and, most hopefully, my sons).

Busy workday at the GUG, decent flow, nothing unusual until I hit the cash drop, which shows more than $30 short. I have no explanation. A report is written up. With Jake on the line, Bob in the lobby, Linnon and then Laura joining me on the registers, Sam at the grill, we show no hitch in our giddy-up. Orders move briskly. Crowds shift through.

After work, I change into chinos and long-sleeve T and walk up toward Black Sand Basin, intending to cross over to it if I can find a path. Instead, stopping to eyeball Castle and the perking Sprinkler nearby, I find Linda from the post office and an older friend, and I learn that, as a volunteer, Linda walks among the geysers and scribbles estimated times of eruption on their placards. I wait with them five minutes, through a promising series of splashes, and then move on.

I become aware, as I pass groups, of the nearly constant gabble, some of it sophisticated, some echoing much of the equally constant gabble in the dorm, and I realize, again, how compulsively expressive and information-laden we have become. Knowledge in, knowledge out. Factoid barrage. Opinion overload. I feel tired just thinking of it. I prefer the near-stillness of another bull bison and his smooth, dusty bare-patch of bed in a grassy snack bar amid the marshes along the main highway, just south of the Old Faithful ranger station and clinic. He lies in a pine-guarded sink within a few feet of cars strumming the rumble strips, showing a languorous mellow (if you overlook the upthrust horns). He doesn't clock in or out, either, as far as I know.

A left turn from the main asphalt path, which I avoid as a runner, takes me, to my surprise, through a stand of pine, curves up a hill and skirts Daisy, not (as I'd thought) a pool, but a geyser, flanked by two other geysers, Giant and Grotto. Mostly steam and a flirtatious splashing. I ascend a curve through more pines and then I spot, crowning a hill ahead, the fluted sinter bowl of Punch Bowl Spring. Its boiling constantly sloshes, creating a stream that curls away downhill. I turn around. Two more geysers, Sawmill and Spasmodic, wait, also quiet. The loudest sound in the basin at that moment is wheezing. Not a geyser's, not a pool's. Mine.

Back in Bitterroot, as I wrestle with the day's purchases (a DVD, a lime Coke) and paperwork, Johnny the floor manager calls out to me and sidles up with my new roommate, big guy with red hair, short-cropped and gelled, and a cautious look and confident grip. Name is Jeffery. So, the window side of Room 207 now has new sheets on the bed and a small rotating fan and a bottle of hair gel and a bag full of clothes, and I return to self-consciousness. No whiners!

I get back from writing in the Lodge just past 9PM, and around 11 Jeffrey strolls in (OK, he just walked) with a young woman in tow. He introduces her as "Afton," and I mention the Robert Burns poem ("flow gently sweet Afton") and chat them up. They go for pizza and (apparently) spirits, and then they come back around midnight and I hear him telling her, "Here's my lovely bed."

They proceed to have sex. In MY room. While I'm HERE.

I feel embarrassed, angry, just slightly amused, a little deadened, the way you do after the first few minutes of a porno movie. The noises aren't sensational—he has turned his fan up full blast as a mask—but I can't sleep and so think about my reactions.

I am not, after all, his prudish Aunt Fanny. On the other hand, they have invaded my space, flouted the rules and act as if I weren't there. Which I emphatically AM.

Never mind the lectures about Sexually Transmitted Diseases and keeping your peter in your pants and the worthiness of real love and all that. I am suddenly put in the position of not knowing when they might come (in both senses of the word), what they will do, when they might leave. I am also definitely pissed off. Roll on, Sweet Afton, roll... right OUTTA HERE!

I am feeling no better when they wake me up again around 6:30AM with another romp (maybe the rickety single bed will collapse!), and so, when my alarm goes off and Jeff finally greets me, I find myself saying,

"You will NOT do this again!" Uh huh, uh huh, he says. "NOT do this again," I say, step into my pants and shoes, pull on a shirt and leave.

I'm talking, I realize, in my father's voice. I wish it carried more of his officer/salesman's command.

At breakfast, I'm joined by a woman named Judy, who's about my age, and, needing solace and maybe attention, I tell the tale. She strikes the perfect balance between compassion and outrage. At lunch, I am approached by a senior citizen named John, former researcher and photographer from Waukegan, Ill., who tells me Judy said I might make a decent roommate in the geezer dorm, Obsidian. The geezer dorm? Talk about a crackling gossip network. Also, about a hidden world, a substrate of supportive Baby Boomers.

Thank you, Judy! Great timing, John! I tell John that my sister, Jean, was born in Waukegan. We go to personnel. We set up the deal. I move tomorrow.

Just like that. Earthquake, geysers shifting, rivers realigning, trees toppling. Well, I only feel that way. For me, it's more like Steamboat (or maybe Geezer) Geyser suddenly showing signs of life. And I might have a full-blown 200-foot blast near at hand.

I think more about the help from Judy. She had nothing to gain. She heard my story, and she reached out to me. I wondered, just then, how often I had ever done that for anyone.

The workday is a tiny but determined Beehive (geyser reference), almost incessant; my cash drop is nearly $2,000, and the crowds include 300 teenagers on a nationwide bus tour. Most of them order a sandwich, fries and a drink. Separately. Many of them use credit cards. Geyser rushes show staying power, and at one stretch the team—today it was Alicia, Brian, James and, later, George—works so well together that, in a lull, we slap hands and laugh about it. No hang-ups. No backups. Very few changes on orders or void-outs on registers. The cliche that a person can take pride in doing well at any job applies here.

FIGURE 1. Simmering, steamy view near
Great Fountain Geyser. *(Ken Hubbard)*

FIGURE 2. A glorious sign and sight after weathering a snowstorm:
my welcome to Yellowstone National Park. *(National Park Service)*

FIGURE 3. Lone Star Geyser—shown here
free from intrusive bison, runners and flocks
of tourists—shows its stuff. *(James St. John)*

FIGURE 4. Old Faithful Lodge, my
haven for writing after work.
(National Park Service)

FIGURE 5. Robert Reamer's Old Faithful Inn (1900), before makeshift rectangular additions for added profits. *(Monterey County Historical Society)*

FIGURE 6. Tally Ho Coach climbing the Old Road from Gardiner station to Mammoth, circa 1906. *(Montana State University Library)*

FIGURE 7. A terrace at Mammoth Hot Springs potboiling against a summer sky. *(GJ-NYC/Shutterstock)*

FIGURE 8. Bison lunching on the flats in Lamar Valley. *(Jim Peaco/National Park Service)*

FIGURE 9. Bison starting their climb from Gardiner to Mammoth along the Old Road. *(Blazing Big Horn Studios/Shutterstock)*

FIGURE 10. Gardner River floods after chewing through U.S. Highway 89 between Gardiner and Mammoth Hot Springs, June 2022. *(Doug Kraus/National Park Service)*

After work, legs already tired, I change and run out on the board-walk again to Biscuit Basin. Before I even cross the highway, I can see that Castle is going off, and it's still gushing and pluming when I get there. An onlooker uses the word "tornado," and he's right: the water column is corkscrewing out, spinning and rolling as it expands and then melts away. On the boards at Biscuit, I see three runners coming my way, a rare sight here. Air fives! To dodge a large group of Russians, I jump onto the ground and back up onto the walk, and one of them looks over and exclaims something. I try not to assume that it's a gibe.

As I return down the concrete serpentine to Bitterroot, my friend the bull bison greets me from his spot. Hello, buddy! Beyond him I see Jeffrey, sitting on the steps with a different girl. I read his look as sheepish. We talk a little with several others in the group about the steam phase at Castle and watching Beehive, and then I head up for a shower and Jeff says he'll be right up.

I open the conversation with, "So about last night…" He apolo-gizes three times. He says that Afton and he were telling each other how they felt cold at night and that they decided to sleep together to keep warm. "We cuddled," he says. "We didn't have sex."

Well, OK, now that I've blabbed that he did to several people (which means everybody in the network knows), I can think back to what I actually heard, kissing sounds, rustling of linens, a couple of what-might-have-been moans, and I admit that he could be telling the truth. I sometimes leap to the most dramatic conclusion, especially when suffering sudden trauma (and lacking sleep). I should just keep my mouth closed, mainly, and talk to the person concerned. Still, about that replay in the morning… No, don't ask.

The main culprit in this case agrees that we could each use room-mates nearer our own age and interests. Coming out of the era that mocked greasy kid stuff (and also produced some of the worst hair this side of the Piltdown Man), I have trouble finding the allure in a bottle of blue goop labeled LA Looks (Sport Look Extreme Hair Gel), or in the odor of Degree for Men, or in Jeff's and Richie's and our other neighbor's carefully arranged body washes and deodorants and grooming aids.

You wouldn't think men would be so sensitive about their looks, about their smell, about their image and their effects. But I've always felt that men have been sensitive all along, at least to a greater extent than popular stereotypes and common sexual assault and violent crime statistics suggest.

Jeff, saying whether we stay together or not he'll come visit and no hard feelings, has taken his contrition (and a young woman) for a swim in Firehole Lake. I am hoping our last night won't be another all-nighter, for BOTH our sakes, because I must augment today's 11:15-to-7:15 with a 7:30-to-3 and then another 11:15-to-7:15. Which means only two meals each of the days. Less nutrition and less sleep be no good, especially for the grammar.

I report the next morning, 7:15AM, lobby. I start to scour. Ron/Ole appears at 7:30 and says, "Oh, I forgot to tell you, I switched you to 11:15. Go home." Which means I won't leave work until 7:15PM Which means I must move NOW.

I mock-strangle him, but inside I am feeling his fretted bulldog larynx under my thumbs.

So I proceed back to Bitterroot, where Jeff is just stumbling out from sleep to suck at his first cigarette. Richie's roommate informs me that Johnny Lopez, a good-humored artist and cook from Oklahoma, had a row with his boss and is leaving tonight, by plane from Butte. He was good with the bullshit but good to people, too, and I am sorry to see him go.

As I leave Bitterroot, I grab some names from the roster posted downstairs. Mine is still among them. Last name first. Some are clearly Anglo; some are these:

Basjgarova, Veronika; Balintova, Lucia; Barna, Bratislav; Boniecki, Pawl; Bredikhin, Vitaly; Cong, Ning (my tall and skeptical friend from China); Gierej, Tomasz; Hao, Chuan Yeo; Huo, Ting-Ting; Kratochvilova, Jitka; Ku, Hsiao-Fang; Li, Li Wen; Liu, Chung-Feng; Paperiello, Rocco; Quibodeaux, Julie; Yen, Hsiang-Ting.

For all I know, some are American-born. But you get the sense of how many of my (former) co-workers have arrived here from overseas, nearly all to earn what money they can and fly back, for school or work. We nearly all have immigrants in the blood. And some say the native Americans started as Asians walking the land bridge to what would become Alaska.

No one seems sorry to see me go, which I do. While bantering with Jeff one last time, I clean out the closet, haul out and fill the Exeter duffel, stack and carry out the papers, pile everything in the car, stop at the stoop to say goodbye to a few people I barely know, and drive away. About three-quarters of a mile. To the dorm called Obsidian. From a vegetable to a rock.

My roommate is now John-somebody. Gray hair and beard, camera nut (loves the 4-by-5 black-and-white plates, the big view cameras). I see him briefly while moving in. Seems like a good guy. Off to work.

Switched back to cashier, I set some sort of seasonal sales record. A smile from a boss, no celebration. Working late, through a steady flow of customers that surges into rushes, I have missed my trip to Grant for the elliptical machine, and my writing time in the Lodge, and my chance to settle into the new room, and I am sour. So what? I must be back at 7:15 to open again tomorrow. I want A LIFE.

That night, my new roommate, full name John Quick, lies down on his double bed in Obsidian 120 with several sharp groans, leans over to turn on his heating pad and says good night, leaving me an hour or so to head to the Lodge to reflect. He's been talking about reagents and about determining the leaching of metals from glass containers in chemical analysis, and about his former boss and former girlfriend, who still work for the drug company in Illinois that cashiered him (or pushed him to cashier himself) after 37 years. Both boss and girlfriend are named Kathy, one with a C. I feel your pain, John.

I grab the laptop and head for the Lodge. At the next table the head of a tourist family says to one of the new Polish workers, "So you're here to chase girls and have a little fun and make money?" Two workers nearby laugh. He doesn't, and I don't, either. But I understand the sentiment. If young men can still peacefully pursue young women (and vice-versa) for sexual gratification and a possible long-term relationship, then fundamental biological imperatives are still at work and we can sweat a little less about sexual politics and gender-bending and the social roles of men and women and the gay-lesbian threat and the anti-gay-lesbian threat. Shouldn't biology and common sense be the guides? If I were a sharp young man from Poland instead of a jaded oldster from hunger (not Hungary), I would look around and see the beautiful and smart young women from Poland (and all the other countries) and consider myself lucky to spend a summer testing the chemistry with them in Wonderland.

The mechanics of that testing, of course, aren't always sublime. Or clear, either. "Enjoy yourself," the family man says. The kid is no doubt ending an eight or nine-hour shift and can't wait to get the hell out of the building. He does have time to assure me, though, that the chipmunk is alive and scrapping.

As a lobby guy again the next morning, I have more time to work with Bob Yeager, listen to his banter, contend with his aggression. I'm learning. He is, in fact, teaching me valuable lessons, including a tweaking of my hyper-sensitive reactions. It's the old lesson of NOT doing; of listening rather than reacting or speaking, of meeting fire with ice. We joust over a man asking me for a tray and my handing him one (in the name, I thought, of customer service), and I hear the phrase so familiar from my years with Kathy, "Let me finish!" He's right. I'm too busy reacting to follow his logic through.

I quickly realize that the customer had seen the trays on tables and figured he should have one before he placed his order, but I had not weighed the implications. If others in line see him with a tray, Bob points out, they will all want one, and the only place to get one on the customer side of the product bank is to pluck a dirty tray from the slot on top of a trash container. "You'll have customers getting sick," Bob says, "and I will not let that happen."

Gotcha. If his method is a little hyper-tense and nose-to-nose, well, why should that matter to me? That's his peculiarity.

I also begin to get a better grasp of gaining confidence in a work-place, and of the value of tolerance, and of not being afraid to speak up while picking the proper time and issue to speak up about.

On the other hand, make no mistake, I consider it a moral crime for these large corporations to bully and hector and underpay their workers for labor that is often deadening. The wider issue in a fast-food place is the personal and social impact of haste and pressure (not to mention the long-term effects of cholesterol and sugar) and, especially here, the toll of our incessant buying and self-gratification. I see happy faces, sure enough, in those burger lines; I also see faces flushed and voices strained with the stress of the big family vacation; of enforced fun without, in most cases, any genuine adventure. Hey, let's all go to that place that's just like McDonald's so we can feel comfortable again!

A drive down to Grant gives me more points to ponder. Surprised (but not much) finally to find someone else grinding at the elliptical machine, a big blonde young woman in jeans who speaks (when I ask her how long she'll be) in what seems like a Swedish accent and says, between heavy breaths, "Thurtee five meenuts." I don't pout but use the time to visit Grant's Yellowstone store, where I buy water and yogurt and talk to the fiftyish guy at the checkout. I tell him I work at Old

Faithful and notice he's from Georgia. I talk about Jack Etheridge, a wonderful judge and fellow-teacher at Exeter and my only connection with Atlanta, and about the Peachtree Streets, saying I think there are seven. "There are 32!" the man says, and when I mention it sounds like a place with a lot of good people he responds with a story. Seems another clerk asked man from a certain city how he liked it, and the man said "I love it! The people there are so warm and friendly." The same day another man from the same city comes in, and the clerk asks him the same question. "I hate it," the man said. "People are cold and competitive."

I've often thought of how I filter the world, how my numbness in recent years has taken most of the sparkle and spontaneity out of what comes in through my senses. That was part of John Berger's point, I think, in *Ways of Seeing* (the book arose, I discover, from a '70s TV series on BBC). We filter everything we see and hear and touch through our own limited senses and experience.

Prompted by the painting of a ship at sea on the dorm wall, I think of Pearl Harbor Day, remembering the generational meaning and how important it was as we grew up. On Dec. 7, 1941, Dad was a sophomore in Mechanical Engineering at the University of Wisconsin. Within six months he was at sea in the Pacific overseeing boilers on an oil tanker with the Merchant Marine, heading into the battle of the Coral Sea and then Midway. He had to grow up fast. Now sabers are rattling again between the U.S., Russia and China, and what we hope (as one commentator put it) is that the sabers keep rattling in their sheaths and no one pulls them out. Now they're nuclear and ultrasonic and carried by drones and stealth planes and missiles edging into space, some of them overseen by fanatics. As Bartleby the Scriviner would say, we should prefer not to. The treatment for this malady? Dunno. Can't see any one formula, though many are offered by religion, advertising, idealists, and the self-servers.

At Grant, I pound at the machine, finally, and afterward, about to press the bar up from the bench, I hit a sequence of thoughts that take me back to 1970-71. It started with Mom's letter saying she had watched and enjoyed the NBA playoffs (I, of course, was deprived), and then I flashed to the pained face of the new arrival from overseas when he learned that there were no TVs here showing the big seventh game (won late in the fourth quarter by San Antonio over Detroit), and then I wondered if any guy in the dorms *did* have a satellite hookup and used it as a lure for women, and *then* I wondered if any guy FAKED having a satellite hookup to try luring a woman to his room.

Me, thinking about a woman in my room? Blame what's left of my hormones.

20
NEW FRONTIER

I step out for work, this morning, into a pink fog. The swirl of subterranean steam from many pipes, the cast of the early sun, the mystery and magic of the forces of Nature have conjured a momentary miracle of color and light. I'm basking, just now. Please don't explain it to me.

The BIG INTERVIEW is set for tomorrow, meeting Jerry Kahrs in Gardiner. I'll try not to grovel. Took me 20 years to learn that the best path to a job is honesty and, beyond that, conviction. Not the courtroom kind but the personal kind. I still want to please people, still want to ingratiate, but I should think first of the 17 years it took me to get to *The Milwaukee Journal.*

I applied for work there nearly every one of those years, and at first, I was told either that they had no openings or that I needed more experience (I kept adding clips from ever-larger papers). Then, one year in the early '80s, I was told that I was close but that they had hired a black woman from Harvard. I couldn't argue with that. I had no clue what she had been through, never read her writing, but I knew that, even out of work, I had more opportunities than she did.

But I *did* learn to argue. After getting a Master's in Journalism and returning to Milwaukee for temporary jobs through Manpower, I applied as a feature writer through a blind box (no I.D.) in *Editor & Publisher*. Surprise! A call came in from *The Milwaukee Journal*. Come in for a tryout.

I was working, just then, as a secretary at the Milwaukee County Zoo. I remember walking from 41st and Center across Washington Park and down Wisconsin Avenue to the *Journal* interview (my car was long gone, taken one night in Eugene by the repo man, and I didn't have much change for buses).

Up in a far corner of the newsroom, I waded through some kind of intelligence test, wrote a sample story from a list of "facts" and earned an interview with George Lockwood, Managing Editor for Features.

Mr. Lockwood gave me the firm handshake and asked what I thought I could bring to the paper. I said I wanted to explore everyday life. He challenged the idea that everyday life and ordinary events are news, and that triggered my fervent defense of writing about what really matters to local people, and about the people themselves. He leaned back in his chair and smiled. All right, he said. Give me a story about the Milwaukee Bucks ball boys. I did, they printed it, and I got the job.

I'm hoping, now, that Jerry will smile, too. I still remember being turned down just last year at a Burger King.

At lunch in the House of Ptomaine, poor James New York is lamenting a second day of split double-shifts, piled on him because he's now a shift lead. Someone says that another of our workers was seen sitting on a bench and sobbing, not to be heard from again.

I have such thoughts about myself (without the tears), not as urgent as before, as I retrace the trail up to Lone Star. The early-up jagged hills flatten me to a walk again, but I make the back half of the five miles in pretty good shape, and the only obvious wildlife are clouds of gnat-like flyers and swarms of ground-hugging wasps or flies in two flat areas just short of the geyser, wing-hum combining to a very loud drone. Lone Star, as usual, barely sighs.

That afternoon the weather shifts, and Old Faithful goes off gray-against-gray. Low clouds, light rain, ragged geyser plumes blowing east and dissolving in the mist. Inside the lodge I look, in vain, for the chipmunk. Basket of pinecones, check. Andirons and broom, check. Decorative grate, check. Little buddy, vanished.

The next morning, I am reminded to replenish the Comment Cards. Take a look at those Yellowstone National Park Lodges cards stacked in their little condiment-side vestibule with pencils alongside and you see the triumph of psychometrics. The Puppet Masters.

The cards ask for a patron's reactions to food and drink, service, cleanliness, atmosphere, and they offer five layers of Likert Scale evals, with cues (italic for the categories, boldface for key words in the sub-categories): 7 Very Much Agree down to 1 Very Much Disagree, and a space for N/A. I consider, of course, the whole card Not Applicable in any sense to breathing, suffering, humdrum, exhilarating reality. But, in this Wonderland, the cards keep marching.

Now, of course, in this digital age of instant REAC-TION-slash-OPINION, we are bombarded by endless invitations to rate products and services, including delivery and deliverers. They want us to do their market research, however ham-handed and simplistic.

Where did all this crap about the measurable mind, the capturable experience, come from? I have some clue: Mendel's research on the mathematics of the gene, Darwin's ideas about natural selection (and categories), triggering Sir Francis Galton and his book Hereditary Genius, Germany's "psychophysics," L.L. Thurston's Psychometric Society and the application of science (fact and theory) to slapping a slide-rule onto human attitudes, beliefs and academic achievement.

No. As the great English poet William Wordsworth wrote in "The Tables Turned," in 1798:

One impulse from a vernal wood
May teach you more of man,
Of moral evil and of good,
Than all the sages can.

Sweet is the lore which Nature brings;
Our meddling intellect
Mis-shapes the beauteous forms of things:—
We murder to dissect.
Enough of Science and of Art;
Close up those barren leaves;
Come forth, and bring with you a heart
That watches and receives.
In today's electronic whirl, my favorite verse is:
Up! up! my Friend, and quit your books;
Or surely you'll grow double:
Up! up! my Friend, and clear your looks;
Why all this toil and trouble?
My answer: greed, fear, envy, habit and insecurity.

The departed co-worker Athena, bless her, seemed almost to live and die by the marks on the comment cards. That electricity, I expect, comes from the spinning of the chain of command. She has moved on to a better place, Mammoth, and she can revel in and agonize over the cards there, too.

I have no idea what the company does with the results. At the working end, I have seen no evidence that they do anything. But ours is a service economy, so maybe a few somebodies somewhere are dancing to a good living on these flimsy little pee sheets.

What they really dance on are people such as Athena, and her boss, Ron, and the wide-eyed and usually amiable (at least to me) Ole, or Roy. And the customers, who feel empowered. And me.

Opinions, some bar-stool wit once said, are like assholes: Everybody has one. But opinions have become a favored commodity in this capitalist system. I have a "take," therefore I am. Grandiose pettifoggery!

Great inventions. Great minds. Not much of that, here. Refined systems, borrowings and stealings, adaptations. An endless churn. We are supposed to act appalled when someone says, "Can I have some McNuggets?" But, hey, look at the chicken bits, what else are they?

Ray Krok is our Ghost of Receipts Past and Present. In the future, we would love to see his methods land in the graveyard. More than likely they will command the mansion, brightly lit. I'm the one trudging back to Bitterroot in the dark.

21

THE KINDNESS
OF STRANGERS

Hope. Not the diamond. Not the town in Arkansas. Not Bob, the late comedian (bless him).

As I've learned almost daily these last five years, hope is a job application. Hope is also a good conversation over coffee on the veranda of the bookstore in Gardiner. Combine the two, and you get... well, something near diaphragm-tickling expectation.

I can already see myself working for owners Jerry and Christina Kahrs in the Yellowstone Gallery on Park Street, in full view of the Roosevelt Arch and Electric Peak beyond, selling jewelry and sculpture and original paintings (and, OK, borderline souvenir doodads a rung or two above the usual Yellowstone and Western keepsakes and send-aways. They gotta make ends meet, right? And the bird kites are cool). I can see myself living in the nice apartment in the basement of their stone-and-shingle home (a bathroom all my own, and a kitchen, and a living room, and an extra bedroom and a backyard that ends at the cliff tumbling to the Yellowstone River), helping them to sell art and plan shows and set up computer programs (shut up—I can *do* that if there's a good reason) and making twice the money I can here.

They would need me until mid-August, ideal for returning to Wisconsin in time for Alex's and Ansel's birthdays and (even better), returning *with* them, since I could bring them out here and put them up in my spacious "guest" room. Even the living room couch looks comfortable.

Jerry and I had a talk that wandered into The Band and Vietnam veterans (he's one) and liberals (he's one of those, too) and handmade goods and the romance of falling in love in Jamaica (which he, from New Orleans, and Cristina, from Boston, *did*—been married more than 25 years) and the joy of particular off-beat and truthful movies and, of course, the challenge of selling enough good art to keep a gallery going in a small, conservative town.

My hopes have gotten themselves up.

That mid-July afternoon I start my run in Mammoth, up the sharp hill and down the Old Road, feeling middle-ish. Clouds have gathered in the north and east, a blessing. I run down past the two tree-lined creeks, past the now overgrown pond, past the dry sink, to the stretch where I can see most of Gardiner arrayed along the river. And then I turn around. Psych! Psych! I am running uphill, sometimes fairly steeply. I am lung-pinching and throat-gasping. And the clouds are starting to spray a cool, slanting rain that shifts to the front, the side, nearly the back as I pound up the serpentine.

Then, somewhere near the most distant piney creek-tumble, I hear thunder. Fourteen people, the record says, suffered injury through the years from bolts at Old Faithful. Lightning flickers. I try to pick up the pace on a hill and don't. I approach a more level stretch, and now lightning flashes. I lift my knees. My legs accelerate. I can see the alabaster terrace now, and Bunsen Peak beyond. Ka-ZZITZ! I am MOVIN' IT!

I wait for the fatal bolt as the road curves, revealing the campers and Army buildings and post office and dorm and hotel and general store below, and I fairly dive at the thin thread of path zagging down the steep hill. MADE IT! Almost. Still have the entrance boulevard to negotiate (a big SUV actually stops for me) and that half block to the parking stall behind the personnel office. Oh, *yeah!*

I celebrate with a bag of Corn Nuts, Yellowstone plastic-bottled water from yesterday, and a half of the steak-on-bagel from lunch with Jerry. Driving back to Old Faithful, I hit serious elk and bison blocks (lots of frisky calves). A busy-but-good day off, and it ends with a welcome chance meeting with Brad and a friend who knows a lot about the Inn and would LOVE to talk about Xanterra perfidy and the rape (from her view) of a beautiful building, and with a look at one box of John's photos, wonderful studies of underlying geometry and movement in rock and landscape and human fabrication. In a reserved, back-achy way, he seems happy to show them. So, I am already thinking of setting up an exhibition for him at the Yellowstone Gallery and Frameworks. I dream of greater things!

After my nightly writing bout at the Lodge (traded reassurances with the Polish guys, put up the chairs on the last two corner tables), I settle in the commons at Obsidian and am joined, somewhere around 11PM, by co-worker George, a mischievous former grocer. I have likened him to Loki, the Norse god described in Encyclopedia Britannica as "a cunning trickster who had the ability to change his shape and sex." Sounds like modern invention to me.

George talks about two near-death experiences: his heart attack, pacemaker and emergency pacemaker replacement, and hitting a bison at night with his Chevrolet. The car was totaled. The bison walked away.

George also speaks ominously about a guy from Mammoth who might be coming down to manage; a guy George steadfastly refuses to work for (the guy MUST be, as George says, a "total asshole," because I've never known George to get down on anyone). He also mentions learning lessons on how to live at a late age, about how long it takes many of us to find some serenity.

Oddly, Jerry and I had talked about the same thing over the burger-and-wrap in Gardiner. He had brought up Jane Fonda, in the Vietnam anti-war context, and talked about her new book, in which she apologizes for what she saw as the unintended consequences of her notorious visit to Hanoi (I thought she was both naive and very gutsy, using the wrong approach on the right track) and talks about regarding life in her 60s as a "last chance to get it right."

Jerry is feeling that way in his late 50s, and I guess I am, too.

I told both Jerry and George my story about meeting Jane Fonda, in Rochester in (I think) 1983 or '84, when she was raising money for the California senate campaign of her then-husband, Tom Hayden. She was known, then, not just for films and her visit to Hanoi but for her exercise videos, which sold in the millions. I was assigned by Keith Moyer, my editor at the *Times-Union*, to chronicle her visit, where she led an exercise class for donors (as it turned out, nearly all women, many between 30 and 60) and two young men. I was the third man, juggling my tape recorder, just trying to keep up. Jane was leading the charge in blithe and vigorous form, instructing all the while in a strong and steady voice, and she was working the quads and the stomach muscles, lots of side-kicking and leg raises, working, *working!*

Around us, the women kept right in step, a few even exclaiming or laughing. I was barely holding on. About halfway through, the two macho guys behind me slunk out. When I approached the autograph and merchandise table afterward for a quote, Jane looked at me fully and brightly, shook my hand and said, "You did good."

When I got back to the newsroom, Keith said he needed the story for page one in 15 minutes. Then he smiled and said, "Take 16."

I had also met Jane's father, in the Salt Lake City International Airport in (I think) 1963 or '64. Much to my good fortune and also to my shame.

When I was 13, encouraged by my father to do something useful, I volunteered to sell poppies for the American Legion and was assigned to the Salt Lake City airport. Being shy, I had to gin myself up to approach passengers as they hurried through the concourse; somehow, I managed. People recognized the poppies and the cause, benefitting war veterans. I was approaching every likely person in sight (emphasis on older and settled-looking) and had just traded a poppy for a handful of change when a guy hurried up to me. "Do you know who that was?" he said, breathlessly. I gave him a bland no, and he said, "HENRY FONDA!"

No, I said. No. I would have recognized him. "It *was!*" the guy said, and he moved on.

I couldn't stop myself. I had to hunt that donor down, and I did. Saw him from behind as he was heading to the airport barbershop, stunned to see that it really WAS himself. I watched through windows as he sat in a barber chair, scolded myself, walked away, walked back. Then...

I approached him in the chair, his face in lather, and, needing an excuse, offered him another poppy. He looked at me squarely and said, "I gave already. I think it was to you." Oh Jesus, you're right, please, I'm so sorry. Pause. Then I held out a piece of paper and a pen from my pocket. Can I have your autograph?

Stoically, he signed it, and when I thanked him, he nodded. I still have his signature in an album somewhere. I never asked for another autograph from anyone.

Like nearly all of my brief encounters with famous people, the memories bring to mind one of the all-time classic story ideas, from an editor at the *Times-Union* whose name eludes me (Phil, I think): "Touched by Greatness." The paper invited readers to submit their anecdotes about meeting celebrities and the famous of many stripes, and it drew (as I remember) the greatest response in the paper's history.

All of us crave significance, don't we? An actual exchange with a celebrity verifies us in some way. Maybe the Greeks felt that kind of rush in touching the robe of Achilles or Socrates. We get autographs and squirrel them away as talismans of some kind (unless, of course, we regard them as manna and auction them off for big bucks on eBay). I like to think that down deep they verify only that these people are successful and, maybe, blessed in some way, while we're not...but *might* be.

Never, of course, have I felt LESS significant than I am just now in the park. I see better days ahead.

I join the (mostly senior) talkers at the breakfast table. They're convinced that I've been shunning them, and they're right. I like my reading table in the far corner, when I can get it. Nothing personal. Just me and Johnny Steinbeck. Just me and Jumping John McPhee. But Judy is there, and, after all, she's been good to me, so I sit and largely listen before finally beating the beak.

We are talking numbers, about 4,000 employees, they say, in the park, including the NPS people and the Xanterra people and the Delaware North people and the YPSS people. About 800 here at Old Faithful. Don't know that the public realizes how many.

Then we are talking access for the disabled. One man at the table, a bus driver/tour guide for the summer, spends his winters back in Jefferson County, north of Denver, driving school buses for special needs students. He might carry five or six, but he has to drive many miles to pick up and deliver them.

I remember, then, one of my students at UW-Whitewater. I can't recall his disability; he walked with a brace, I think. I remember that he was bright and eager and wrote a good story about a barbershop back home. Chicago area, I think. I remember even more clearly his girlfriend, who had cerebral palsy and a guide dog, a big golden retriever.

When I talk about her, how smart I realized she was, how aware, the bus driver's face goes red, and he daubs at his eyes.

Then a short blonde sits down; I see her coming. It's Marie, bossy impresario of the Lodge dining room. Only her name's not Marie. It's Edith. (Where did I get "Marie?") And she's a master quilter. Teaches it back home in Ohio. I am revising another assessment. Still don't like her style. Gruff. A little pompous. But the woman has skills. She's also history, because I am LEAVING.

22
TIMMY
TUMBLEWEED

This last day at work in the GUG seems long, busy enough in spurts, plagued as in recent days by a balky computer (I spent the first hour as a runner, finding it much easier to talk to the fry cooks through gaps in the product ramp) and still somehow becalmed and benumbed.

Departures do not reprise arrivals; they are not vivid with first impressions and the anxieties of incorporating new faces and tasks. They have been, for me, always sad, in different degrees. This one not so much. Ole wants me to stay to closing. On the last of seven straight days of work, at the end of nine hours, I just want to find the fresh air. He doesn't push.

I am not King Arthur in "Camelot,' asking, "What do the simple folk do?" I don't believe folk are simple, for starters. But I find myself after these three months in light bondage thinking of my grandparents again and of the many, many men and women (and children) who work long hours in difficult conditions for little pay and just keep on. We get better, sure. We can experiment, in small ways. We can lock onto novelties, as I did, to finding and keeping in the cash drawer one of the new buffalo nickels, or focus on amusements or escapes after work as ways of getting through the day.

Or we can just let our minds go, give in to the routine, take one moment at a time, try to stay clear on the only slightly varying detail in the box-car rush of them and the slow empty spaces of them, try not to allow music in our heads beyond a single simple tune (today's, for me, was "I'm 'Enery the Eighth I Am"), or thoughts of our distant loved ones or any others beyond the flash of someone we might want to love, or past regrets or concerns or excitement about the future. We can rest later.

We can also pay better attention to the people around us and with us. In the course of the day, I take my co-workers' pictures. Not all of them. Linnon has called in sick. Alicia is gone back to Texas to have her baby and maybe get married. Athena has long-since moved on to Mammoth. Jake, the runner I call "Flash," is off today (the other Jake, brighter and more thoughtful, is working the cooler).

Bob is off, too. No Ron/Ole, either. But most of them log in. I try catching them on camera as they work, no posing. But they nearly always see me and look up or produce a frozen smile.

Still, their bodies are bent and their hands are busy. They will leave for other things, Craig to return to school at Cornell, Greg to the Montana State theater program, Laura to…well, I'm not sure (I picture her singing somewhere, in the Ivy League), George to his part-time, post-retirement grocery work, Adam to…not sure. He reintroduced me to "East of Eden." I picture him doing something thoughtful. His weight works against him, but his mind is buoyant.

Finally, in the midst of a rush, Craig takes a picture of me, in action, in uniform. I think of the one shot of me in my Drake University marching band outfit. Good to have one, if I can ever find it again.

As Craig and I and later George and Ole (he reappears) and the Polish and Czech cooks work through the orders, I can observe that

I've become pretty efficient. I peel the last fallen fries off the floor, pull out the last 24-ounce drink cups, the double-cup coffees, the clear plastic waters, grope into the cooler for the last Frusion smoothies and fruit punches and Old Faithful Ale, issue the final "Hi, can I help you over here?" and "You can get fries and a drink with that in the combo" and "That'll be $22.36" out through the autonomic smile, tap the last orders onto the screen and run the last credit cards through the slot and field and disburse the last curls of receipt tape, and I feel only a twinge of regret that the skills will go (mostly) unexercised. I finish with a $2,519.90 day. I have given them their money's worth.

I leave after counting out and shaking Ole's hand, firm grip, both smiling, and collecting my book and apple from the locker and running my card through the time clock one last time. The clock flickers and beeps. The hallway in Subterranea is filled with cold fluorescent light.

As I emerge into the evening, Old Faithful is going off again, and I love watching it on a relatively calm night with the sun low behind it. The central steam column is dark gray, pierced by silvery freshets, each one new, and as the clouds rise, they take on the sun's bright light.

I reach home (soon to be another previous address) in time to submit a change-of-address card at the Old Faithful post office and to collect my mail. Before heading to the rec center for a last turn on the new elliptical machine, I read the letters.

The first bears the hard imprimatur of the Dane County Child Support Agency. The headline reads:

NOTICE OF INTENT TO SUSPEND, REVOKE OR DENY LICENSE(S)

This is followed by... "to enforce the child support lien filed on the court case listed above (1395FA000095)."

They can snatch away my driver's license, they say, but will not if I "pay the lien amount in full or make satisfactory alternative payment plan arrangements with the child support agency." I am asked to call Cindy Richmond (the name has been typed on whiteout over SANDY KANHALD) in Madison at (608) 266-4031. I think I owe something like $1,300. So I will call, and this is a chance to amend the last conversation I had with these people, which ended with me trying to explain my situation, bouncing back off a brick wall of two impossible options and saying, in frustration, "So basically you don't give a shit," and the woman at the other end hanging up. Sandy? Sorry.

This time my options are clearer. I can tell them the circumstances of the missed payment (the firing in Yuma) and my time of unemployment. I can tell them that the court garnished 60% of my wages in my last two seasonal jobs, hardly enough to live on. They don't care about my situation. They want payment. So, I will focus on finding a reasonable amount, and if that doesn't work, I'll have to go back to the lawyer who handled my bankruptcy, if she's available. Got to keep the emotions in check.

The other three letters, in one envelope, are from the boys and Kathy.

On killer-whale stationary imprinted with his name, Alex writes:

> *"Dear Dad, How are you? I went fishing with Uncle Peter. I didn't catch anything and neither did he, but his friend caught a largemouth bass. My Aquatic Biology class is also really fun. We finished our survey of Lake Mendota and are switching to Six Mile Creek. I'm starting to get ready to write the required paper. Also, on July 5th, two days from now, the new maps for Halo2 are coming out! By the way, rats are sooo (insert the boys' word for excessively cute)! Love, Alex"*

On the Garfield cartoon cat stationary imprinted with his name, Ansel writes:

"Dear Dad. Hi! Hope you're having fun! Sure is great down here! Great weather (especially in the basement). By the way, we got Xbox Live! Man is it awesome. Learned lots of new stuff on my trumpet and tennis is going great! Have you re-strung my racket yet? By the way, I got a new one, a Head Intelligence "Smart Racket" or something. Liquid metal. Also, I'm giving the Busse's tennis lessons once a week (Alex Friday, Erik Monday) to the end of the summer. The Busse's got their fourth Halo2! Sincerely, Ansel."

No superlative will tell how much I miss those kids, how much I wish we were together. Kathy's letter reminds me why: She's desperate, can't find work, could lose the house. What's wrong with me? Nothing a king's ransom wouldn't fix.

I look around the lodge's dining room for the last time as a regular. No more hard-oak-and-herringbone-wicker chairs. No more looming stone fireplace. No more little chipmunk or mouse scampering for crumbs. No more geyser shadows flickering the sunlight.

Then, as I am closing the laptop in the glow of the hearth, I look up one more time to see Veronika, coming toward me.

I tell her that I am going up to Gardiner, and she says that she's glad for me. Then we have one of those cinematic moments, where secrets are revealed as the movie ends. We do not talk about attraction or intimacy. She simply tells me that, as a teenager, she was raped, and I can see that it left lingering scars, physical and emotional. All I can say is that I'm sorry to hear that. At that moment, I take it as an explanation for not touching each other.

Alone in Obsidian Room 210, one last night, I visit the screw-top physician and his colleague, Dr. Pepper.

In the morning, after dropping John Quick's (and my) big empty Bacardi bottle into the recycle bin, my last EDR breakfast is taken with

Bill, a school bus driver from Grand Lake, Colo., and Mike, co-author of the waterfalls book. We talk about the Inn, and about Xanterra's odd media postures. Mike recalls appearing in a documentary about Yellowstone's waterfalls and says the company informed him that he could not appear in his company uniform. How, he wonders, would that association reflect badly on the company? Too personal? Then Mike recalls the situation in 2001-02, when the company signed up hosts of workers from overseas and then, after the World Trade Center cataclysm, hit a wall in processing overseas visas and hired a second group, only to have the first group flood in when restrictions were eased. "They had some people living on cots in the rec center," Mike says.

Maybe the company can't afford to care. Mike recalls the arrival of a devout Muslim woman from Turkey. She finally lands a room, and he takes her over to it. She meets her roommate, who has been busy. The whole room, he says, is plastered with photos of guns and other violent images. The current resident has built a monolith in the center of the room, entirely of beer cans. "I felt so sorry for that Muslim girl," he says. Let's hope, I say, that they came to terms…or swapped roommates as soon as they could.

I decide to take a last run toward Biscuit Basin. I will appreciate the indifference of geysers.

I start out at good pace, legs feeling light and quick because I didn't stand on them for hours yesterday. From the road behind the O.F. Inn, I can see a geyser going off—Castle? I cut in front of the Hamilton Store and its wooden bric-a-brac facade, past the gas station, across traffic and onto the cinder connector to the asphalt path.

Castle is only steaming. What's going off is Grand.

I run fast enough to get there with 10 minutes left in the show, which seems especially good. Jets of water fly up and off at angles like components of a firework, drawing oohs and aahs from a hearty crowd. Each fusillade seems stronger than the last. Then the jets and steam fall suddenly back into a placid pool. I stare, remembering Dave's description: if the water doesn't drain, a second burst is coming.

The pool holds. I tell a few around me, "It's going to go again." It goes. The first bursts might be the highest and widest of the day. The crowd AAAaaaahhh's. We look up at a wide effusion of droplets, big and silvery, and some of them fall on us. After another few minutes, it suddenly subsides again.

I start to walk north, about to resume the run, and then look back. The pool has held. I stare, waiting for scalloped edges to show that the drain is open. They don't. The surfaces shimmers and is still. Seconds later, BOOM. A THIRD eruption! One older man in a safari hat prances past me showing the amazed and delighted grin of a little boy.

I resume the run, navigating the down-curving boardwalk across the river, and… Whoa. Riverside is going off! Sidereal plumes, water on water. No rainbows, but a damn good show. I keep up the charmed run to the Basin parking lot—it bulges with vehicles—and, seeing throngs on the Biscuit Boardwalk, I turn around. I feel strong to the last hill up to Old Faithful, when I labor. A good, tiring time.

In the dorm, my key surrendered, one of the last people I see, striding theatrically toward me, is RJ. Of course!

"Hey, how about a hug?" he says. That's in his routine. I start in about the Norwegian ancestry, absent the hugging gene. Then I say, what the heck, and we hug. I'm not bad at it. He has a lifetime, apparently, of practice. Still, I much prefer the awkward hug with Dave.

I drape the last shirts over the suitcases in the trunk, slide my violin atop the window-shelf above the back seat.

Vanished, as if never there. No more Tim Wisconsin. I'll discover my new identity shortly.

I drive back up to Gardiner at nearly 50 m.p.h., most of the way. Darkness closes in. I make it to Gardiner Market in time to buy cherries and coffee and a steel pan before they lock the doors, and I regard the town after nightfall, lit by neon from motels and bars and strings of pale streetlights.

At the house on Park Street, lights glow in the windows. Jerry and Christina have returned from Bozeman. At the open front door, Ellie the golden retriever noisily introduces herself, then subsides into a gentle nuzzle. She was named, I learn, for the Beatles song, Eleanor Rigby. The cats, both black, are the smaller Sassy with a patch of white on one paw and Aesop, or Big Easy. How could I fail to like a cat carrying the nickname of Ernie Els? Well, I'm not, true enough, a "cat person," but I can try. I must watch them, I am told; they are known for jail breaks out any unguarded aperture. J and C look a little tired. They are sorting baked goods and organic cheese. I am introduced to some of the exigencies of commerce: tomorrow, Jerry has to sit down with the representative of a credit card processor to untangle a mess caused when somebody left a digit off a long series of card numbers. The night air is still warm.

At the back door, showing me the porch light, Jerry recalls a similar night looking above the line of hills to the north and seeing the shimmering coruscations of aurora borealis. You gotta like a guy who gets into a sight like that.

23
THE RIVER

On the eve of my new life, I try a (now) familiar run: the dirt trail threading the north edge of the canyon of the Yellowstone River.

Across its 3,471 square miles, Yellowstone Park proper is ribboned with waterways, some 2,172.52 linear miles (the Yellowstone Spatial Analysis Center tells me) of creeks and rivers, including the Firehole, Madison, Lamar, Gallatin, Lewis, Gibbon and the scenic Snake, coursing through the Grand Tetons and Ansel Adams photographs. A few conjoin as headwaters of the mighty Missouri, joining the Mississippi at St. Louis and on to New Orleans, to the Gulf of Mexico and the Pacific Ocean. Other Yellowstone streams go their own water-way across the Continental Divide, headed for the Atlantic.

The Yellowstone River is the heart of the park, and beyond. Among other things, it's the longest undammed river in America's lower 48 states, 692 miles. It showcases the Upper Falls and the mighty Lower Falls and its grand canyon, pushing on from the sprawling Yellowstone Lake east through the Hayden Valley and north to meet the Missouri in North Dakota.

Most likely, the name Yellowstone started with the Minnetaree (Hidatsa) Indians, who labeled it Mi tse a-da-zi; Rock Yellow River. They passed the name along to French Canadian trappers, who passed it along to the explorers, Lewis & Clark, who condensed it to Yellowstone.

For me, on a renewed (and rejuvenated) run above the Yellowstone River's rim, everything becomes blessedly simpler. Over the deck truss bridge, past the Absaroka Lodge, up the steep Jardine Road, down the precipitous dirt connector from the LDS church to the well-beaten trail, heading east, I smell sage on the bracing air and exult in a feeling of freedom, in mind and limbs.

No slide on slippery rocks today. I *know* you! I feel as if the trail knows me, too. Welcome home.

24
SQUIRM BY DOING

First day at the Yellowstone Gallery and Frameworks, under the watchful eye of pleasant and seasoned co-worker, Elenor. I learn the rudiments of cash register, packing desk, cleaning routines. I apply price stickers and, after unpacking them, fix metal light-switch plates to a cork-board display.

Elenor Kovacik Graff is a kind of artist-in-residence. Her stained glass tryptic of a soaring mountain peak stands atop the large stone fireplace (and it attracts more attention, Jerry laments, than the inventory). She quickly shows me the value of information. Each set of objects in the store has an artist or two behind it, and their stories and detail on their techniques make those objects more vivid to the buyers. Sure wish I had a better memory.

The day might be the year's warmest, somewhere in the 90s, so the ice cream shop up the street (Raccoons) shows a packed porch. Jerry envies the income, but I picture the chaos inside, the lines backed up, the sweat and fuss, and I am grateful for native American flute music on the sound system and the occasional wandering customer.

At one point Jerry apologizes to me for showing stress, though I have hardly seen it in him. Of course he feels stress. They need to make, he says, something over $2,000 daily to keep the business healthy. They take in something over $800 today.

I *do* enjoy the company behind the counter: the dogs Ellie and Buddy. They are old and a little overweight, and yesterday they struggled a bit in the heat of the afternoon, though they didn't pant as loudly as a few customers. But they seem sweet-tempered and tolerant.

So many little things to learn. Here's the key to the shed, where we keep shipping boxes (in six sizes) and plastic popcorn and packing tape. If anyone asks about a giclee print, the giclee process captures the image of original art on film or digital bits, cleaned and framed by hand. Here are the keys to the glass cases, one set in a drawer in front, one set hanging from a peg in back, and each case opens differently. You don't need a box for an embossed ornament; boxes cost 50 cents apiece. Save those for jewelry. Just use bubble wrap. Navajos generally press and glue their stones into place; the Zunis use inlay, more painstaking. These miniature mountain scenes are hand-cut on a jigsaw. Try to keep kids from playing with the display boxes (of course, you can't). Extra copies of prints are stored here; clear plastic envelopes are kept over there; mailing materials are stored back there. Make sure the scuff rug is kept flush against the front door. Water the flowers in the street boxes twice a day, and clean the bathroom at least once, and make sure the dogs have enough water in their bowl in the back. This knife blade is made of 27 individually applied layers of stainless steel. Unwind the hawk kite from its pole out front when needed. Here are the 16 steps to tallying and double-checking the day's receipts. Turn off the swamp cooler upstairs. Switch off the lights (14 locations), lock the back door, open other interior doors, turn off the sound system, and prime the alarm. You have 20 seconds to leave the building.

Don't forget Ellie.

I feel pressure not just from customers, of course, but from Jerry and Christina and their staff, Elenor and Jonie, to GET IT and to get on with it. Of course, the greatest pressure is coming from ME (damn me!).

Every new worker can feel overwhelmed. I think of the football quarterback analogy, where everything seems to go so fast at first and then to congeal into a satisfying slow-motion, a vigorous ease. I had reached that, in the end, at the grill. But this kettle of flopping fish seems a lot fuller, and the selling of art objects bears little relation to the schlepping of burgers and Old Faithful ales. I've barely scratched at the art of selling. The key, Christina says, echoing generations of entrepreneurs, is how to read the customer and close the sale. Can't hawk art, as opposed to burgers, with a glad-hand and a smile. Knowledge first, then passion, then fake it until they take it.

As new customers enter, I am aching with self-awareness. Questions should not be answered with what Jerry (referring to herds of exhausted tourists) calls "the zombie look." Daze of the living dead. "Uh, gee, I dunno" doesn't go too well, either. I decide on, "Let me ask Jerry."

There is beautiful stuff here. Beautiful stuff. Astonishing tromp l'oeil landscapes in oil and acrylic, animals hand-carved from antler horn, Carter Gowl's dazzling Ilfochrome views of Lamar Valley and the Absaroka range, handmade silver pendants and bracelets and earrings, hand-woven rugs, packs of Haynes postcards in their original wrappings. Jerry is afraid that the world, or at least the non-wealthy, non-powerful, non-overeducated part of it, doesn't want beautiful stuff, at least not enough to cultivate and pay for it. I am afraid that he might be right.

Still, he can look out his front window at the Roosevelt Arch, and at a breathtaking mountain-scape beyond. Jerry and Christina could have wedged their store into the congeries of galleries selling to the well-off and wannabes in Jackson. This is a better, more rooted, more genuine place. It's just tough when most people genuinely don't want, or when they look don't see, what you offer. The lament of artists and their disciples.

25
KEEPING TRACK ON THE TRACKLESS FRONTIER

August has brought heat and drought. I've had nearly three weeks in the gallery, now, and I'm a slow learner. As Elenor and Jonie have warned me, Christina is a stickler for detail (she needs to be) and sometimes impatient. Jerry just needs another good salesman, somebody who can read background and persuade customers and who knows the inventory and its connected human stories.

I'm falling short on all counts.

Maybe I'm thinking too much about the still-unfinished piece on the Old Faithful Inn, or the story on handmade Yellowstone signs sent to the *Jackson Hole News & Guide* in Jackson, or I'm *farmisht* about any possible future in newspapers.

Ducking the pincers of the paycheck, I am pinched, nonetheless.

I picture Jerry hunched over the calculator, toting these up. Here's the tally from Friday, pay period 08/01/2005 - 08/15/2005:

Hours: 71.5

Rate: $8.00

Amount: $572.00

Deductions:

Social Security: $35.47

Medicare: $8.30

MT withholding: $5.00

NET PAY: $523.23

YTD: $2,384.00

Social Security: $147.81

Medicare $34.57

MT withholding: $17.00

NET PAY: $2,184.62

From the $523.23, I immediately take $125 for child support, $75 in rent for Jerry and Christina, $30 to cover the bounced check at the Sinclair gas station, $50 for the credit card (not nearly enough), $50 for back taxes, $50.14 for groceries, $45 in pocket cash. I am clinging, now, to $191.91, and I know I will siphon off more for groceries and, possibly, gas in the next two weeks.

To get ANYWHERE once work ends, I'll need at least $200. To return to Wisconsin, I might need $300, and that's arriving with almost nothing in my pocket, trying to find a room to rent, hauling the belongings out of storage, pounding the pavement again to find work.

Tough titty. Get busy, bud.

I scramble to finish the story on the Inn, begun in June, and to send it off to newspapers. As if they'll leap at it. No circular file needed, now; just a fingertip on the *delete* button. Still, I have to test the rust, try the market again, even knowing what I know, even with the scars of recent experience still burning.

Here's the lead:

YELLOWSTONE NATIONAL PARK, Wyoming. The moose is dancing again, the bears bellied back up to the bar, the bell-hops buzzing through Bat Alley, the army of room attendants and waiters and helper/guides back on the march.

This weekend, they'll return to rest. The building around them won't.

The Old Faithful Inn, most storied building in the history of America's national parks, swung open its red double doors July 1, halfway into the season, without ceremony. Occupants were crowding the threshold.

Despite ballooning gas prices and Hurricane Katrina, the Inn, just a curve of boardwalk away from the celebrated geyser, was booked solid through its 101st peak season.

That season ends Sunday (Sept. 11), a month earlier than usual. A three-and-a-half year renovation will continue throughout Yellowstone's often ferocious winter, and it will postpone next year's opening until at least June. The full May-to-October run, scheduled for 2007, may not resume until 2008.

Regardless, demand for rooms has never been higher. As long-time guest Dianna Kellie of Anaconda, Mont. says, this is not just a summer rental. It's a national treasure.

It's also a century old, made largely of wood, and standing on some of America's most dangerous ground. Though the rest of the park (save for its bugling bull elk in rutting season) is quieting down from a reasonably busy summer, the next month will literally blow the roof off much of the inn. Project manager Chris Martison of supervising A & E Architects of Missoula, Mont. says that more than 50 carpenters, roofers, plumbers, electricians and engineers will scramble to replace rotting roofs over the lobby and dining areas and lay in long-term floors, upgrade pipes and wiring and fire safety features and install quake-resistant structural steel, all before winter closes in.

Not bad, hope to get back to it.

Jerry has me back in the office picking figures out of the daily reports, the sheets where we scrawl the record of each transaction, item, dollar amount, means of paying, whether we're selling a product or framing or shipping. Even that ongoing daily record, to my mind, is a needless duplication. Isn't all of that on the computer, with backup? Now I am breaking out totals on another sheet, one day at a time. On an adding machine, I total up sales by means of payment for inputting into the computer. Few of the totals add up, and I'm dulling over. I head up to Kevin's gift-and-latte emporium for a 12-ounce dark roast, room for half-and-half, and, as I'm standing there, I hear a familiar voice on approach and there's…

Veronika. "I wondered if you were still here," she says, in the Slovakian English, and she smiles the Pepsodent smile. I give her a hug. She is up here for the day, job finished, shopping, awaiting a flight (tomorrow? Saturday? Somehow a man is involved) out of Bozeman, headed back home.

She turns away to browse the racks; she was always turning away to some duty, and I head back to the gallery. As I walk through the door I turn and there she is, just behind me. "I was hoping you might be working today," she says.

I want some romantic moment or at least some bubbly optimism, but this isn't the movies. Veronika, instead, starts to bewail her hard duty in the Old Faithful Lodge and the Snow Lodge, her low pay and long hours and paucity of warm fuzzies from management (hey, girl, welcome to seasonal work!) and the fact that she'll get no rest and will have to start school nearly the moment her foot touches the tarmac at the airport.

She has, as always, no great interest in me. I am the audience. But I appreciate seeing her, the hug, the chance to wish her well. No tender backward glance.

I have been brought to ground, meanwhile, by Kevin's mention that he ran the Old Road yesterday and just flat-out breezed! "I felt really good," he says. Uphill was easy. Up-and-back seemed short. I congratulate him, as my ego squinches (especially after that miserable run on the self-same road last Sunday), and I realize that I've been kidding myself. Absent other runners, I can see myself as stalwart, hard-working, skilled. In truth, most real runners would kick my ass.

At the moment, my future in Gardiner seems poised for an ass-kicking, too.

I find, as I get back to the apartment, a duty list shoved under the door, as a reminder:

1. Greet customers.
2. Observe customers.
3. Cleaning tasks (and its sub-categories)
    *   Vacuum daily
    *   Vacuum upstairs frameshop
    *   Empty all waste cans
    *   Keep the assessment area tidy
    *   Empty contents of all boxes
    *   Dusting (a constant chore)
    *   Tidy displays
    *   Keep the Zapotec rugs in order and displayed properly
    *   Clean Mylar sleeves of photos and prints on display
    *   Keep the front sidewalk swept and clean
    *   Water outside plants
    *   Keep the bathroom clean
    *   Keep the glass countertops clean

- Use the duster to wipe down framed items displayed on the walls
4. Unpackage and check in arriving merchandise.
5. Unpackage and check in arriving merchandise for frame shop.
6. Place barcodes on items and put them on display.
7. Process arriving merchandise, prints and posters.
8. Keep poster tubes stocked.
9. Keep jewelry boxes stocked.
10. Keep plastic bags stocked.
11. Be observant at all times.
12. Be acquainted with all art media and crafts.
13. Learn how to package things thoroughly and quickly.
14. Acquaint yourself with shipping procedures.
15. Computer duties as assigned.
16. Check displayed items and make sure all items have a barcode or price on them.
17. Phone Sales, message inquiries:
    - Make out an invoice for sales.
    - Take down complete information *and* read back details.
18. Learn by doing. Even when there are other co-workers on the job, try to complete a sale with a customer without relying on your co-worker.

Gimme an OY! Gimme a VEY! Gimme an UFF DA OY GEVALT!

At least they included 18). I remind myself that none of this is about ME. It's about the business. And in that arena the whole place is in trouble. I remind myself that, whatever my shortcomings, they need me. And I need them.

In mid-afternoon, during a lull in customer traffic, Jerry is filling out and paying insurance bills. Car insurance. Health insurance. Home insurance. Business insurance. If he could keep all the money he pays on insurance, he says, he and Christina would be rolling in it. He comes up with a figure: $15,000 a year. *Wow*. How did this happen, he wonders, this accumulation of material THINGS, this accretion of responsibilities, this onslaught of commercial harpies? He remembers when he swore never to own more than he could carry on his back. He was happier then.

So, I mention balance, and I mention that if he had simply stayed on the road, he would be living at best half-a-life. And, of course, the road keeps changing, and the vehicle keeps changing, and the guy IN the vehicle keeps changing.

He understands all that. He has a Hopi word for balance (*Hozho*) that brings in good habits and good work and good friends and generosity and occasional joy. He feels too far on the other side, into the worries. He has the damn computer to goad him; later he shows me a screen with a colored bar graph of monthly sales for the last three years, and 2005 is coming up short on nearly every bar. Without a more fulsome August, he wonders how they, how *we*, can keep going.

I pore over the list that night. Then I visit Dr. Bacardi and his colleague, Dr. Pepper, and they assure me over the rim of the mug that I will remember every detail and perform like a champ. First thing the next morning I forget to plant the paper osprey on its pole out front to flutter in the wind and catch customers. Working, *working!*

26
ON THEIR WAY!

They're coming!
After much negotiation (and, maybe, their mother's weariness), Alex and Ansel will be flying into Salt Lake International for a weeklong visit. For the first time since watching *It's a Wonderful Life* at Christmas, I get tears in my eyes.

Jerry, for his part, vows to be a new man. Here's a guy who's putting in 10 and 12-hour days (sometimes 15 or 16) and facing down the gun barrels of creditors and tax people and needy employees and artists and other vendors, not to mention the power and water and phone companies, and he's man enough to acknowledge his own failings and go to work on self-improvement. That impresses me.

He also tells me that he talked to Kathy when she called the other night, sharing her concern for the night trip the boys and I face to Salt Lake on Saturday, and that he'd be glad to let me off early that day so we could travel in daylight and offers to loan me the money for a motel.

This is a *good* guy.

I drop my car at the Tire Iron for its pre-Salt Lake servicing, and on the walk back, my hamstring barks a little (though not as loudly as

Ellie, who greets me from the front door). I think about athletes and moments such as mine, on yesterday's second lap down on the Gardiner High track, when some part of the body changes course, often with just a subtle twinge or pull. Imagine training for the Olympics and, in the week before competing, sensing a noodge like that, feeling it sharpen, realizing that it might ruin four hard-built years, even a lifetime, of sacrifice and effort. But, even after tragedy and failure, we DO keep living, keep reporting for duty.

To keep living, I keep writing. Time to tackle the story on the lettering in classic Yellowstone Park (and, by extension, nearly all National Park) wooden signs.

I had started the story in Mammoth, from a suggestion from Melanie Moroney, and carried it to Old Faithful and back north. One sign reference still makes me smile and wince. On the Grand Loop Road between markers 9.5 and 7.5, just south of a quiet meadow (unofficially called Whiskey Flats) is Whiskey Flats picnic area. Yellowstone Park sign maker Virgil Hall gave up making "Whiskey Flats" signs when 18 of them were stolen in less than two years' time.

America the Lootiful.

I had visited Virgil's shop in Mammoth, spent time exploring his work and life, and, first in the Snow Lodge and then in rented moments at Raccoon's, chopped out a story about him. From Raccoon's I send it to the *Jackson Hole News & Guide*. An e-mail pops in from the wonderfully named Johanna Love. They are going to print the story! They will send me a check! Here's the start:

MAMMOTH HOTS SPRINGS, Wyoming. Guy walks into a tavern in Bozeman, sees a sign up over the bar, WHISKEY FLATS. Recognizes it right off. Made it with his own hands, saw it go into the ground at the Whiskey Flats picnic area north of Old Faithful. Federal property. Knows darn well somebody stole it. Says nothing.

The next sign that went in was bolted to the ground. Somebody stole that, too.

Same guy walks into a sign-maker's convention in Las Vegas, finds himself surrounded by well-wishers. He is, he discovers, a legend in the business. They all seem ready to toast him, with whiskey or otherwise.

With routers and carving knives, brown stain and white paint, Virgil Hall is adding his last installment to the legend as September ends. He can't seem to go quietly.

By e-mail, by phone, by walk-in, they are coming at him, still coming at him. A Montana guy wants a template for rustic lettering. A woman from California needs help with a varnish.

The man's retiring, for cripe's sake, can't you ease up?

They can't. And if the school kids from Gardiner or Yellowstone Elementary or the local Cub Scout Pack happen by, well, retirement or not, he'll trundle them in and take them on a tour.

In Yellowstone National Park, he points out, every sign has a purpose. For the last 38 years, Virgil Hall's main purpose has been making and repairing and replacing those signs, thousands of them, often under pressure.

Now he is signing off.

On Oct. 1st, Hall retires, joining his wife, Madeline, in a lakeside home in Washington state. At age 62 he leaves reluctantly, expressing the worry that no one will step in and care for the signs as he has; that nobody will continue the craftsman's line and the lettering that most viewers connect instantly with the nation's first and best-known national park.

(He is relieved to learn in late September that the National Park Service Personnel Office in Mammoth is issuing a call for his replacement, and that they will call on him to help with training. To find where to apply, look outside for its identifying sign, made by Virgil Hall).

"These are my babies," he says. They are also among the most famous signs in the world, especially the much-copied pair bracketing Old Faithful.

Cartoonists at Warner and Hannah-Barbera, among others, have toyed with those. The authors of Bugs and Yogi never got it right, Hall points out, and today's big-time TV commercial makers don't, either (possibly fearing a challenge to copyright, though neither the park nor its signs have one).

Where the signs show most, though, is in snapshots. Millions upon millions of them. Later that morning, for instance, modes of transport from skinny minis to mammoth blubber-buses would be pulling over at the park's five entrances, or at one of the six enormous Continental Divide signs (the park's biggest), acting out the ritual:

One or more figures leave the vehicle, trailed by one more. They approach the sign, turn and, in shifting postures, array themselves, then freeze. The trailing figure, sometimes gesturing like an orchestra conductor, raises the camera and... another sign lands in the family archives. The sign-swarmers are more numerous around the signs reading Old Faithful Geyser.

Most of those signs came from Virgil Hall's hands.

Hall can get an Old Faithful or any other Yellowstone sign almost exactly right and from dead reckoning, without stencil or measuring tape; almost, as he says, in his sleep. He's glad to share the recipe, and to warn any would-be apprentice that he took 16 years to perfect it, learning from the best in the business.

The carpenter shop at Mammoth is a long pale yellow industrial building with a low-hanging, red-shingled roof, and the lights in the sign shop inside pop on one recent morning at 5. Hall has spent much of his waking life there.

In the next room, six electric fans whir in chorus. The smell of paint and shellac is sharp. The routers stand ready in a rack. The back wall is papered with thank-you notes from grade school kids; they drew out signs of their own, and Virgil carved them, errors and all. "They deserve to see, to keep their own work" he says. "That's a great beginning."

His final major sign lies across a tabletop in a side room. Here's how he made it: Score the wood with a knife. In the letter wells, paint wells is puckered, giving them a weathered look.

Nearby, he is putting the finish on a few of his last projects: three gray IDs for hot pools and one final arrowhead, for a retirement farewell. Not his.

The signs, like their maker, have integrity. They are not trying to sell something. Yellowstone Park, through travel agents and online barkers, through commercial video-makers and tale-tellers of all stripes, through its unbeatable brand name, has already been sold.

The signs have informed or coaxed many millions of visitors. The most famous identify a celebrated site. Some, with arrows, offer directions. Others, the ones Hall considers most important, issue a warning. Beware of fallen trees. Take notice of a fire zone.

Please take notice, too, of the man who makes them, by hand. No machine, he says, hopefully, will ever match the eccentric art or the eccentric self of the sign-maker.

Virgil Hall should have better tributes, but I suspect that the one he values most comes from his family and friends. Just now, I have NO better tribute than finding a story of mine in print, byline and all. I'm back in the biz!

In a spirit of celebration, I push into running gear (the Waukesha Trailblazer Half Marathon long-sleeve, the purple UW-Whitewater shorts, the New Balance 603's, the sweat-stained Velocity Sports Performance ball cap) and lope toward the Old Road.

I think, momentarily, of an ex-Marine running friend of Jerry's, who had stopped by this morning to rattle off numbers that turned out to be his quarter-mile and half-mile interval times. (They didn't overly impress me, but the guy is my age, and I'm sure I'd be hard-pressed to match them). He is training for the Marine Corps Marathon later this summer in Washington, D.C., his first. I'd gladly go along just to see a Nationals game. I ask a few questions about his training but am smart enough not to get into marathon lore. As I tell Jerry, running talk is a universal sleep aid. Tell me about your last race. Oh, and could I have a pillow and a Scotch and soda?

I head out behind the Xanterra buildings and my legs, free of long days standing behind a cash register and running fast-food errands, feel springy. The road snakes away from the North Entrance ranger station and up into the foothills, and I am walking in the first half mile. No interval times here!

I smell the sage, and I notice as I examine the bushes that their leaves explode upward much in the way that geysers do, with shoots reaching up and angling out. I wonder at such harmonies, at how they might work in us. Does a sense of nature's wholeness or union congeal?

I am trying to explode upward, too, but all that congeals is my center of gravity, which seems to gain weight as I slog upward. The road bends and twists and elbows, ribboning a moil of up-slopes that rise more than 1,000 feet in five miles. The lower portions seem toughest; I walk at least five times, using the next bend as another launching point. I'm barely jogging.

In places, though, the Old Road forgives, offering stretches of welcome level and even a couple of brief downhills. I attach myself to distant groves of dark pine, marking freshets of snowmelt that, on this hot afternoon, seem almost spent.

The air is hazy with dust, or smoke. Jonie, on a brief visit to the gallery that afternoon, has said there's a fire to the south, somewhere (probably) in the park. Later, at the food store, the woman processing my groceries would recall 1988 and the night the fire came over the mountain, threatening the town. The grasslands I am traversing, she says, helped stall and stop it.

I take each curve and switchback as it comes. The legs continue to feel strong; the lungs ache a bit, the breath harshens. I reach and pass a second cordillera of pine, recognizing a creek and surrounding marshes as a place where I was wary of bears, and then see, on a high ridge ahead, the lone pine with a crown spreading sideways, like cedar. I spot two more on otherwise bare, stony hilltops. The area reminds me of an island in the Aegean Sea. Finally, I crest the last steep hill, and the white sepulcher of Mammoth's lower terraces rises before me, an apron for the many-hued Bunsen Peak beyond. (Big run; I'm feeling heroic.) Five miles in.

I stop at the rim of the Mammoth plateau, scanning the human geometry of old Fort Yellowstone and the newer Park headquarters and hotel and restaurants, gas station and restrooms, and Robert Reamer's Prairie Style bungalow spread across the landscape, like a painting. Explorer stands on his catamount. Can't claim this for any monarch, though, unless it be King Kommerce or Her Majesty the Department of the Interior. I lift my cap and wipe sweat off my forehead with a long sleeve, noting a couple of pedestrians looking up at me. Then I turn and head back down.

At first, on a steep portion, I feel twinges in the right calf and become aware of the foot plant. I'm landing too solidly on the heels, so I shift a little forward. The tightness eases. I can lengthen the stride, here, and I sustain a pretty good pace. First set of pines passes; second set; third. I take the brief uphills easily. Amazing what a few days of relative rest will do. Soon enough, I put the last pines behind me, and I am down into the drylands. The wide crown of Electric Peak overshadows a landscape worthy of any gallery display or calendar page or living room wall. (For those who *have* living rooms.)

Looking across a wide, roughly oval sink and its swale of marsh grass, I set eyes on a lone pronghorn, feeding in seeming contentment. At the sound of my footballs on the road's crunching dirt the pronghorn looks up, and I make a few reassuring sounds. "Hi! Hell-OH! How are you?" as I did with the deer in the woods in Wisconsin and might with a very young customer. The pronghorn stares, then dips down again to feed.

Suddenly, from maybe 20 yards beyond the antelope, a coyote breaks out of the long green marsh grass and heads up the hill, looking back at me. He is furry and almost plump, unlike nearly every other coyote I've seen, and I wonder if he's a wolf. But the muzzle is narrow and the tail puffed, and I just don't see wolf in him. Regardless, he heads over the hill, and I credit myself with saving the pronghorn.

Wait 'til the boys see this place!

27
THE DOUBLE-A BOYS

I have driven through the potato fields and volcanic wastes of southeastern Idaho and the mountains of northern Utah to meet Alex and Ansel at the Salt Lake International Airport. Big smiles, happy hugs, light luggage. We arrive at Yellowstone's West Entrance in darkness, and on the highway lit only by pale headlights I scare them a little by mentioning bears and bison in roadways. The lights of Gardiner seem like Christmas.

When I tell people that I have never had trouble with either son, that we are always happy to be together, they usually offer a slight smile and downward brows. C'mon, man, that's bullshit.

Most people don't know that I left Alex and Ansel at ages four and two, moved 75 miles back to Milwaukee, and that I saw and sheltered them only on weekends, until I left town for short-term jobs out-of-state and didn't see them for weeks at a time. Always, though, I cherished our time together, exploring museums and local attractions, walking in parks, running a few races, and I think they did too.

With work waiting the next afternoon, I take the boys back south through the North Entrance and along the Gardner River's tumbling rapids to dual parking lots. On foot, we find the waterside path to

Boiling River. Three years after our first attempt, we are finally taking the plunge!

Aahhhhh. Steaming rivulets from the Mammoth terraces cascade into the Gardner River where pools collect against rough, handmade barriers of rocks. A mother and her young and skeptical-looking son (from Sugar House, in Salt Lake City) are our only companions, and we ease back against the splashing hot tumbrils and bask. No hot tub comes with scenery like this!

I leave the boys playing video games for a new day's work which starts ominously for me, as Christina assigns me to return sample frame corners to the vast array that's Velcro-ed to movable wallboards in the back of the gallery. I can find very little order in the way the hundreds of samples are arranged on the boards, and I manage to replace, oh, four or five before customers beckon.

In some kind of harmonic convergence, they keep beckoning.

One couple from the Chicago area quickly test Jerry's vow about how to treat customers. The man steps to the counter, amid other business, and says he has a problem that needs resolving. He and his wife (a pretty woman with red hair) had bought a Zuni inlay necklace the previous summer, liked it, but were later taken aback when several of the stones popped out. They need…something. Repair? Refund? Oh, and they had forgotten to bring it.

I wait for the old, tired Jerry to respond. Instead, the cordial, generous Jerry answers that OF COURSE we'll make good on it. Just mail it to us and we'll try to find the artist for a repair or be happy to replace it with something similar and to send it along, no charge. I can SEE the couple relax, and soon they are shopping.

The accompanying lesson, taught at the gallery daily, is not to judge by appearances. I first see the male customer as the aggressive, take-charge type, who wants to take his money and run. Instead, he proves solicitous and patient with his wife and generous with everyone concerned. He ends up buying more than $700 worth of jewelry, including a Zuni necklace for their upcoming anniversary, which we happily box up.

Then a Japanese family comes in and the lesson repeats. The wife wants to try on watches from several cases. Not sure. Not sure. Then the husband wants a look at that silver eagle inlay watch that seems to have lived in a front rotating display case since the Roosevelt Arch was dedicated (1903). Not sure. Show me this other watch here. How about this amethyst necklace? Can I try on that eagle watch again? Oh, and my daughter would like to look at this bracelet with the mercury dimes. And is THIS one made with real buffalo nickels? Not sure.

Amid strewn boxes and second and third go-rounds, I think of Jerry's general lament about Asians, that they love to look and hate to buy, take big chunks of your time and don't spend a, well, buffalo nickel. I know he's wrong about this, of course, though on eyeball evidence I might start to think that Koreans, especially, rarely buy anything. This is a short-term, bigoted view.

With a nod, then another, the Japanese family buys the eagle watch, and the mercury dime bracelet, and a horsehair watch, and the amethyst necklace, and a set of earrings to boot. They spend more than $500, and as they leave, they shake Jerry's hand, then mine. Namaste!

An older couple in cowboy gear buy two large prints. A woman with major convictions about buying goods made in the U.S. purchases painted feather earrings made in Montana. A younger man from Italy picks out that rare pre-Nazi postcard with the swastika, a native American symbol then. Cha-CHING!

We take in, on the day, more than $2,700, and Jerry treats me to coffee. We are smiling. A GOOD day.

I arrive home to find Alex and Ansel absorbed in a review of the myriad cars showcased by their Xbox computer game (Project Gotham Racing). They seem to think I'll know the differences among the various Ferraris and comparisons between, say, the Pontiac GTO and the Dodge Challenger. I murmur something about V-8 engines. And which do I think is better, they ask me, the Pagini Zonda or the Lotus 340R? "The 1964 Buick Special station wagon," I tell them. You go with what you know.

In the remains of the day, Alex stays behind to set some kind of record in Xbox racing and Ansel tests his newfound tennis skills (and the racket borrowed from Kevin) against his *paterfamilias* on the courts east of Yellowstone Elementary, in the NPS residential area below Mammoth. Elk droppings decorate the school's lushly emerald lawns, a startling sight against the straw-yellow of dried grass covering the nearby foothills.

While I'm busy being impressed with his new power, Ansel acts as if he's playing like an elk-dropping, growling, muttering, chopping at the air with his racket and inveighing the tennis gods: "GRRRR! YOWWW! WHY am I so PATHETIC?"

I'm tempted to see the behavior as wages of a perfectionist parent (also my favorite excuse), but I decide to lean on the basic elements of harmony and respect (saving the lesson on learning how to have a good time for later, since I'm still working that out myself).

Sometimes we lose a point, I suggest, because the other person has hit a good shot. Sometimes we lose a match because the other person is just *better*. Wailing about our own poor play demeans their shot and their effort doubly, by denying its quality and making oneself the entire focus of a shared enterprise, by denying the person who produced it. This makes me sound like a preachy parental dip-shit, but he hears me.

Meanwhile, from the first serve, my right shoulder has ached sharply, leaving me to hit soft serves at ear-height, but I DO engineer a few good returns. Ansel loses at least one game with double faults, something patience and practice will iron out. The rest is his urge to hit thriller-diller-killer shots rather than just keeping the ball in play. I tell him that I am not holding back, as I sometimes did with him, but am going all out, and that truth seems to mollify him a little.

More happily, we venture up to Mammoth's Upper Terraces and enjoy walking the boards near the steaming lip of Canary Spring, which spills its overflow in a livid stream (one that joins Lower Terrace runoff into the Gardner as the Boiling River). Then we spy a rougher path, marked in stones, and follow it up a calcite ridge, skidding as we go. We're rewarded with the view of a set of terraces bubbling and piping away beyond the eyeshot of tourists wheeling by on the road just below. Ansel may complain about long walks, but I love watching him react to the sights. He really SEES them; he has the lively eye, and when he likes what he sees, he shows it.

I realize that I want both boys to like what they see everywhere here, and to show it, to gratify my fatherly aspect, I suppose. But I work not to betray that. As I return to the gallery's demands through the afternoon, the boys take a raft trip down the Yellowstone River, tumbling through rapids, and they come back enthused.

Jerry has suggested that I take the boys for chicken fried rice at the Woky-Panda, or whatever the Chinese place is (Wokking Panda), so I do. Eight bucks. Good price, but ouch! We return home, open the cartons, and about then the toilet explodes.

The boys had plugged it, and we had stopped at the Food Farm for a miniature plunger. I stupidly hand them the plunger and point them to the potty.

I hear Alex first. "UH-oh!" Then Ansel. "DAD!" Then the water, splashing in a great oval to the floor. I picture Excelsior Geyser. I discover something more akin to a massive mud pot.

What a display! The floor—Christina's pristine tile!—is awash in fecal matter, spreading around our feet and toward the carpet beyond. Bits of shit and soggy, fragmented toilet paper swirl near our ankles.

I exclaim. I fulminate. "Get towels! No, *out!*" I seize the tiny plunger and ram it through the cess-wash in the fetid bowl, pistoning at the stoppered hole. "OUT! Get a bucket! Get cleaning stuff! Call 9-1-1! AND DON'T LET CHRISTINA HEAR YOU!" If she so much as catches a whiff of this, I'm thinking... All of us thrown out on the street, putting our woeful shoes to the dust and leaving shit with every step. Oh, the humanity!

The toilet, apparently stunned by my onslaught, flushes cleanly. Wading across the floor, I throw towels at the problem, every one from the stack Christina has left on a stand at sink-side, and scramble to dump them into a large plastic bag (my dirty clothes bag back-up) and duck-walk them to the washing machine. Need more. Grab my own towels from the cubby and perform a rude wipe-down. I graduate to paper towels and then to toilet paper. A dry, clear floor finally starts to resurface.

Then I hear Christina in the hall. Seeing she's engaged in laundry, I go ahead and blurt. She responds with a smile and the suggestion of some kind of orange cleaning concoction, and I recruit Alex and Ansel to help. Alex has wisely plucked the wool rug and saved any permanent ruin. Soon the smell of shit is smothered in citrus. At the finish, Ansel says, "This is BETTER than it used to be!" He right.

Jerry comes up behind Christina, also smiling, and says, cheerfully, "Shit happens!" I see, clearly, that the only real problem here is ME.

In the morning, to my surprise, Alex asks if we can work out in the Absaroka Motel's "annex." Sure! He gives the recumbent LifeCycle a spin while I scissor away at the elliptical machine, and we trade sets of bench press.

I work three hours, with a welcome set of triple-digit sales, and then we pack (rooting every Beanie Baby from its hiding place). As I gas up the car, the boys, without balking, stop at the gallery to say goodbye to Jerry. Stout lads!

We pass through the Golden Gate past 2:30PM, accompanied on the Buick's sound system by the melodious soundscapes of Dvorak's "Symphony for the New World," and we traverse the meadows and marshes and the sulfurous spewings of Norris to Madison Junction, where we turn for the West Entrance…for us, an exit.

The highway unwinds again through its changing landscapes. We pass the log arches of ranch gates, the elongated triangles of potato storage sheds, the bunched streets of working towns. Changes in geology and topography seem far more massive and elaborate than I remembered.

We achieve Salt Lake and its International Airport. In the cattle chutes at the entrances to Concourses A and B, Ansel is picked for a frisking. This intensive search is the practical alternative to cavity-searching everybody. Is it one in five? One in 10? One in 25? He suffers the manual pat-down and an intimate wave-around with an electronic squealer. I'm wondering how young they go in similar searches? "Sorry, ma'am. Show me what's in the diaper."

Thanks to one evildoer in Boston tucking explosives into his loafers, meanwhile, we ALL have to take off our shoes and drop them, with our metal items, into the gray plastic tubs. I can't help thinking that the Al Qaida planners have long since moved from airplanes to other transport, to trains, ships full of oil or shipping containers or passengers, convoys of trucks, jammed-up freeways at rush hour, or on from the World Trade Center to other significant landmarks, the Golden Gate or Brooklyn bridges, one of the Washington memorials or government centers, the Statue of Liberty. No doubt the most radical and deluded will find something more creative and surprising to destroy. Fort Knox? The Space Needle? Or maybe, a paranoid might muse, they will move to water supplies, and gasoline farms, and the food producers and distributors. In other words, to pipelines. I can only hope that sanity and human understanding will prevail over anger and fear. I think of Rodney King in 1992, a year after his televised beating by police, pleading "People, I just want to say, can't we all get along? Can't we all get along?"

The boys and I, just now, are getting along into the immediate pipeline, the funnel from waiting area to boarding ramp. We have waited most of an hour, and now the woman at the microphone calls Alex's and Ansel's names. Unescorted minors, apparently, board first. The man assigned to them is extra polite, even when we fail to produce Ansel's boarding pass (the frisker took it, I tell him) and he has to run somewhere for another.

Finally, he proffers an arm and says, "OK, time to go." We are center stage, eyes of other passengers on us. I give Ansel a big hug, then Alex, and they both hug back. As I watch them disappear into the chute, Ansel moves on resolutely and Alex looks back, over his shoulder, and gives me a wan, half-smile and a wave (I read them as rueful, but of course I want them to miss me at least a little). Then they're gone. How many hundreds of times have I said goodbye to them, given them a last half-hearted wave, felt my heart and stomach sink? I walk back, numbly, through the terminal, up one escalator, down another, through the car rental area, through the parking garage, back out along a curved drive to the long-term lot in full daylight and onto the road.

Out along the Wasatch front again, benumbed, I pull off in Layton for an Egg McMuffin and coffee and $22 in gas. I'm hoping that will be enough to get me back to Gardiner, but I doubt it. I'm left with about 10 bucks, payday a week and a half away.

What I've lost just now has nothing to do with money.

28
NEVER REALLY ALONE

U p the Old Road, feeling commensurate. Very dry and a mile high, hotter than most days at 4:30PM in the hard sun, but nothing like the wet heat of Florida or even the fierce dry heat of southern Arizona.

You know it's gonna be a tough day when… (Sorry. I'm supposed to be helping Jerry with a more positive "You know it's gonna be a GOOD day when…") you're huffing on the lower flat. Brisk wind in the face, dust scudding past the ankles. Southern flow packing heat.

I am gasping through several orifices on the Old Road's first serpentine, you know, the old joke about "I heard three people wheezing, and they were all ME," and by the second, a serious triple-swerving uphill, I am lucky to make bend number two before walking.

The alpine panorama unfolding above should allow me to lose myself. Seen from almost any perspective other than our own in this Western setting, we're animated specks, tiny figures in a Promethean landscape: Electric Peak to the immediate west, the Gallatin Range accordioned to the east. The foreground is grassland topped in stands of Douglas fir and blooming sage, silvery lupine, arrowleaf balsamroot, perfume for my nose.

Unfortunately, there's the chest-rattle. And the breath rasp. And the heart hammer, seen and felt from the proximity of eyeglasses bobbing on the nose bulb. And the busy wind in the face.

The upper sink has dried even more. And the antelopes are absent. I plan to run to the second line of trees, to the cattails hugging the snow-melt stream there, but then I see a white shirt and a guy stepping ahead of me, and still possessed of a little false pride, I don't want to turn around just as I reach him. So we trade inanities and I hit the next hill, and the one after that, over rocky and graveled ground, and finally, Mammoth's great white head heaves into sight. I pass the hiker again on the way down, and he calls out. "A lot easier this way!" and I call back, "Sure is! Take care! See you soon!"

I am lying. Breathing is easier, but the quads and hammies and joints take a certain pounding on a long downhill, and I can't relax. The sink is still missing its antelope.

The wheezing geezer routine interferes with serene contemplation and selfless merging with the rhythmic wilds. I keep on, of course. Yesterday, after all, I sat on my can. I don't cowboy up, but I don't wall-flower down, either. I'm grateful not to remember every past effort on every sinuous elevation, so I don't chide myself (too much) for walking where I used to run. Clearly, though, I've faltered some since mildly pulling the hamstring. I try to huff and scuff into the sage and pine and to lose other reference. No signs here. Somewhere around mid-course I cross the 45th parallel, the line of latitude exactly halfway between the north pole and the equator. Somewhere before that I leave Montana and enter Wyoming.

At the top, having approached near enough to see steam rise from the white whale's nostril and whisk away into the wind, I scan Mammoth's settlement from the very edge and see elk reclined on the lawns, overseen by the magisterial bull and his unmistakable crown. Vehicles still crowd the lots, though the cost of their fuel nears $3 per gallon. Pedestrians still shift among the buildings. In what might be the tour's only concrete thought, I wonder when the last of the students from Europe and Asia will be going home, and figure that some have decided to stay on. Later that night, I'm ordering a cheeseburger basket at Helen's Drive-In ("Home of the Hateful Hamburger").

The next day, Labor Day, we await our own high drama in the gallery. The magic word is "Elderhostel." A busload of free-spending seniors, we're told, will feed at the Park Street Grill and descend on the Yellowstone Gallery for dessert. Last year, Jerry and Christina have said, they nearly mobbed the place, asking, testing, picking, proffering objects by the dozen for packing and paying, sending the staff on a dizzying two-hour scramble…and a euphoric toting of receipts.

This year, the elders arrive in small groups, spend less money, and don't linger. Sorry, J. and C. They send me home early.

The following afternoon, warm day, *surprise!*, I am happy to discover Jennifer Anderson waving at me from the door of the gallery, Dave and Danyon close behind. They DID come back from Tower, where they'd been camping, and from a hike up Mt. Washburn. Christina shoos me away right at four, as scheduled.

The Andersons are going to take me to dinner. First, I have my run along the Yellowstone River, and Dave and Danyon follow in a walk. The terrain is much drier than it was during my first few runs over that rocky, rolling trail on the north bank, but I find that I can ascend the hills and recover well, and my walking is brief. I'm in better shape! I pass, among others, a guy with a backpack, two other men (one of whom says, "Didn't anyone tell you how hot it is?"), and a young couple walking two dogs. All of them look at least reasonably happy. I turn around at the marshes where Bear Creek tumbles down to the river in a swath of green, and the run back feels strong.

I pass all of the aforementioned again, and the last is the lone man with the backpack, whose name turns out to be Dana, and who turns out to work for the Montana National Guard and to be walking the path with the two other men I've seen. Dana tells us that one of them, Tom Sanburg, tall and lanky and square-jawed, lost his son Adam on the river a few weeks ago. I blink. I remember the story. Made the national news. This is the father of the Boy Scout who was swept down-river and, presumably, drowned. Tom lives in Helena, and he has been coming back nearly every day to walk that trail and look for his son's body.

I try to imagine that: the need for it, the sadness of it. I flash on losing track of a young Alex and Ansel in a dark and crowded Shedd Aquarium in Chicago (Alex wisely walked to information desk, and we found Ansel, finally, in front of the shark tank) and losing them again, slightly older, on paths in Wisconsin's Kettle Moraine east of Whitewater. I can still summon the overwhelming anxiety and urgency. I knew that trail as a mid-race stretch of the Ice Age 50, and I was running counter-clockwise to their clockwise walk. Spring growth had blurred the view, and I hadn't thought of side-paths. When I ran the full loop and didn't see them, I ran it again in the other direction. No boys. I walked down to a nearby farmhouse, and they called 9-1-1. As I ran the loop in futility one more time, responders mobilized. The county sheriff had come in with a new kind of ATV, narrow enough for the trail, and as he headed out on a last effort I asked to come along.

About a half mile in, we crested a hill and looked down to see, coming up the path...ANSEL! He was carrying a painted turtle, and he stared and then glared at me. As we took him aboard, he said, "Where were YOU?"

Turns out that he and Alex had seen a side-trail familiar from a previous visit, taking them down to a small lake, and had found the turtle with a fish-hook in its jaw, which they gently removed. Ansel and turtle had headed back. Alex had stayed put, waiting patiently at the lake. As a deputy was picking him up, we crested the last hill to see, in the parking area at the foot of the trail, an array of more than 20 emergency vehicles with lights gleaming, shining in the sun. The authorities had, I learned later, called in a helicopter. Ansel took one look at the panoply, groaned and ducked under the front cowl of the ATV, still hugging the turtle. Alex arrived and shyly smiled. After congratulations and thank-you's, we drove down to the lake and dropped off the turtle.

Tom doesn't have that support out here. As he takes off his shoes, he asks if we'll be coming back along here, and I say I'll be doing the trail every week. He says that in some ways, after this amount of time, he might not want to see the remains. Then he says, "I'd appreciate it if you could keep your eyes open for him." Sure, I tell him. You bet I will.

On the way out, Jennifer tells of another son lost in another river, for weeks, and of the mother coming to water's edge and crying out that everything was forgiven. His body was found, Jennifer says, the next day. I would like to help Tom find his son, even if his son's life is gone. Not knowing is the worst.

The Andersons and I adjourn to the local Chinese place, for various dishes involving shrimp and beef and leeks and rice, and then to the chiropractor's ice cream/smoothie shop, where we meet his daughter and his Polish employee (who, I am not surprised to learn, works three jobs to about 70 hours a week). I get the King of the Hill, which has four kinds of fruit and Ginseng. Good food, even better company. Just what I need.

As I run up the Old Road the next morning, I'm reminded that I am not king of THIS hill. What I really need is a harbor, not just a port in a storm but a place of my own. I've been lucky to land here, but the terrain is shifting again. Ready or not!

29

INTO THE
MORNING SUN

Clouds build. The air cools. Not long after I reach work, Jerry tells me that next week will be my last. I've already seen the slash mark in my row over Oct. 1, a week from Saturday, end of the monthly schedule. End of my line. So I say, as I do often, "OK. Sure." And I thank him again for rescuing me from fast food.

The day comes. The morning brings a methodical breaking of camp. I drop the stack of books into the Exeter duffel and haul it out into a light rain. I center it in the car's trunk, follow it with the soft English suitcase (picked up in London in 1980, on my honeymoon with Lynn, after British Airways dismantled the hard case I had inherited from Dad) and the gym bag (given to me by the wonderous Amy Johnson in Rochester in 1983). I tuck my freshly cleaned clothes in the large plastic bag (handed to me in my first day at Bitterroot in May) and press it onto the other bags, then insert the laptop, wrapped in the salmon terry towel and the small, corded rug from the bedroom chair in Mom's former trailer in Baraboo, and my violin in its case, never used here.

Everything seems to connect to something that's vanished.

I vanish from Gardiner about 9, after saying goodbye to Jerry and Christina. They both smile and seem slightly embarrassed, and I smile and DO feel embarrassed. I do my best, thanking them for their generosity, offering one last comment on Jonie's combination of fierceness and sensitivity (Christina refers to her, aptly, as a "Steel Magnolia"). I should never have lost my temper with her, despite her prickles. I should have seen that a spat over swearing or even telling the truth doesn't matter as much as opening outward, not retrenching. Also, I can't live in the shadow of "shoulda" and "coulda." Another lesson.

I have scrambled to leave the apartment as clean as possible, but I'm sure there is fault to find and am glad I won't be there to field it. I hand them my drawing of the Lombardi poplars, slipped inside a thin Priority Mail envelope I cribbed from the Gardiner post office. They don't open it, which I also appreciate. They deal, after all, in fine art.

I shake Jerry's hand and he hugs me; Christina shakes my hand and I hug her. I'm grateful for my time with them, through all its complications and my shortcomings, and I am glad to leave, looking forward to seeing friends and family.

As I start to drive onto the entrance to Yellowstone, I think of playing music and remember that I've left my tapes behind in their blue tub. Then I realize I haven't put gas in the car. I hurry back into the house, pluck up the tub and head back out, unnoticed. One goodbye was enough.

At the North Entrance ranger station, I see a familiar face under a porkpie Stetson and say goodbye. Her name is Carrie, I discover, and she is also from Wisconsin. She has long dark brown hair and a beautiful smile, one I've seen a dozen times heading onto and returning from the Old Road, and I want to talk more. Can't. Vehicles back up behind us, and I tell her to take care of herself. I wonder if I should write to her from the road, invite her for custard, maybe, on her return to Badgerland, if I make it there myself. Nice idea. Won't happen.

Up into Mammoth, I drop off a letter to my friend, Susan Mandl at Yellowstone's post office and try the road to Tower, only to see that it's closed. The reason quickly becomes clear. As I climb toward Golden Gate, the rain turns to snow.

It will stay that way, varying in size of flakes and intensity, all the way through the park, past the Tetons and out through Moran Junction, swallowing mountains. No scenic splendor beyond the marshes past Mount Washburn; no Grand Teton or Mount Moran, just the slightest rocky upsweep and mist ascending to the heavens. Snow thickens on the pines, lays a ridge between tire tracks, collects on the windshield wipers. I slow for a large herd of bison moving toward me in the oncoming lane near Madison, snow clumped on wooly backs and flat foreheads, and I offer a prayer to the weather gods for a merciful winter in the buffalo regions...and for those solitary old male bison, rejected by the herd. If only in spirit now, I am with you, brothers!

The heights of the Yellowstone Plateau slide behind me. I am road-bound into sun-glare across Wyoming's dry hills and flats and through a phalanx of wind turbines for a visit with my brother Tom and his family (Kathy, Jonathan, Kate) south of Denver. Then I'll press on to Wisconsin, to another life. To the next other life.

The page is turned, the new chapter opened. Tragedy? Comedy? Adventure.

30
RETURN TO WONDERLAND

The new chapter might be a book of its own. Back momentarily to Mom and her trailer in Baraboo, desperately wanting to pay my way, I renew temporary holiday work at Lands' End in Dodgeville, Wisconsin and an apartment in Mount Horeb, Wisconsin, then sign on as a reporter with the weekly *Mount Horeb Mail*. I am scrambling to write 10 stories a week and to give them style and substance. I am covering town councils and wading into countryside in fresh snow for a good photo, still sending packets of vita and clips into the snail-mail and online ether.

One afternoon I field a phone call from Mary Jane Fine, features editor of the *Herald-News* in West Paterson, N.J. They held onto my résumé and clips, and they want to fly me in for a job interview and tryout. I win the job and write feature stories for two years there and at the parent paper, *The Record* of Bergen County. I also fall in love with MJ, and we move to Vermont and then Florida and then Connecticut. Long story, left for wider space.

Since Mary Jane and I married in 2009, I had wanted to give her the personal tour of Yellowstone National Park and Gardiner, show her where I had come from when we found each other. In the summer of 2013, the time has come.

I book a flight from Providence to Denver and a room at the Old Faithful Inn. Flight fine, hopes high. At the car rental we are led to a Yugo cracker-box, last car mid-size or below at the moment, they tell us. We pilot the Yugo up a swarming I-75 through Denver's northern suburbs and out along Fort Collins and Laramie and onto I-80 west and then (much better) U.S. 287 northwest, feeling only a tinge of foreboding.

We've seen the headline:

Government Shutdown Looms

Surely, surely the political grandstanders will settle before their self-spawned catastrophe hits the economy and citizens.

I should know better.

We stop for an overnight in a motel near the University of Wyoming and then bunk at the Pronghorn Lodge in Lander, poke into a few art galleries and chow down happily at the Cowfish Restaurant. We decamp the morning of Oct. 1 on U.S. 287 for a stop at the Wind River Trading Post and on to Wonderland.

The route features one of the most spectacular windshield views in memory, the turn around a curtain of foothills into the full glory of the Grand Tetons.

We head north at Moran Junction (what a view!) to Yellowstone's South Entrance, and we arrive at mid-morning.

That's just in time to see park workers hauling wooden A-frame traffic barriers across the road. CLOSED, their signs bark, until further notice. No-no-no-NO!

Little choice. We head down to Jackson, find the last room in a three-story motel along the strip west of town, have a little breakfast across from one of the Elk Antler Arches downtown, poke into a few art galleries. But, no, too much traffic, too much commerce.

Where now? I know the western sage to call: Dave Anderson. "There's a great place," Dave says. "Thermopolis."

I know the name. Dad had once sold two boiler systems near there for Babcock & Wilcox, and he called that area "the real West."

Weather worriers warn of a snowstorm building into the Rockies, but we're committed (or possibly should be).

The drive back through Lander and up through the Wind River Indian Reservation, Northern Arapahoe and Eastern Shoshone, ushers us to Wind River Canyon, a showcase of ribboned sandstone, shale and gypsum with a dizzying drop-off to the water.

We land, then, in a working western town. Oil, cattle, machine parts, tourism. Not Wonderland but, in its own way, wonderful. On the first late afternoon we discover Big Spring, billed as North America's largest mineral hot spring (by volume), and we drive up into Hot Springs State Park, where a ballyhooed bison herd hides from us.

The next morning, with our motel-keeper's urging and, under darkening skies, we wind up a dirt road to what looks like a warehouse and crane to read the sign:

Wyoming Dinosaur Center and Dig Sites

Through the door, hallelujah! We find a treasure-trove.

Starting with the earliest fossils, the progressive Walk Thru Time along the walls displays plants and animals as they evolve through the eons, single-celled protozoa to, the center proclaims, the only archeopteryx, the winged dinosaur, outside Europe. I haven't seen a better introduction to natural history and evolution for curious kids or deprived adults. Inside a glass-fronted lab, men and women in light clothing work on freeing fossils from their rock beds. Standing in mid-floor is the spectacular skeleton of a Supersaurus, a couple of stories high, 106 feet long. This could be the envy of any natural history museum, and nobody paid us to say it.

Back to lunch in the Safari Restaurant of the Days Inn, we discover Wyoming Whiskey, distilled just a few miles up the road in Kirby. It's edgy and peaty, almost Scottish, flavor all its own.

We end in the Hot Springs State Park Bath House, granted to the state of Wyoming by treaty with the Arapahoe and Shoshone on Chief Washakie's condition that, in proper hours, everyone can come free of charge. Blessings to the chief..

We're alone as we ease into the hot mineral water from Big Spring, steam rising around us, and a gentle snow starts to drift down. A moment from romantic fantasy.

Late that afternoon we are hit full blast by reality: Winter Storm, Atlas, the first-ever "named winter storm" (another pyrrhic triumph of marketing). Snow plummets and swirls and hammers past the motel's outdoor spotlights through the night. The next morning, we borrow a shovel to dig out the car, and we're told that Wind River Canyon is closed. Nobody in or out. Extra day at leisure while legions of workers clear streets and highways and fight to keep electricity and water flowing. We toast them with Wyoming Whiskey.

In the Yugo, buffeted by wind, we drive back the next morning through the canyon, just reopened, skittering in the tire-tracks of a truck ahead. Please, MJ, don't look down!

In late September 2016, we try Yellowstone again. Same drive north and west, stops in Laramie and Lander and the Wind River Trading Post, past the grave in Fort Washakie of Sacagawea, Lemhi Shoshone, savior of Lewis & Clark, and on to the South Entrance.

No barricades. Room at the Old Faithful Inn, third floor in the east wing. Plain label, close quarters, too hot. Gift shop OK, restaurant food third-class. One night was enough. On to a place that I knew well, not from staying but from workouts in the exercise shed: Absaroka Lodge in Gardiner.

We step out on the room's small balcony and look across the Yellowstone River and its gulch to Jerry and Christina's backyard.

Over the bridge, east on Park Street, we walk around to the front and knock on the door. A woman answers. Stranger to us, house-sitter to them and, after I explain my history, welcoming. Glad to see that they are still here, hoping they are OK. I can see that they'd enlarged and improved the house; the Grand Canyon painting still gleams in the living room. I leave a note, sorry MJ and I missed you, thanks again for your kindness and tolerance.

I don't hear from them again. No need. We are bound for the same finish, moving at our own speed in our own way. Cheers and Au revoir.

On our way to Old Faithful, we spot our first herds of bison and tourists pulled over to ogle and photo-shoot them, and I say to MJ, "Wait until you see Grand and Castle!" She smiles and says, "Uh-huh. And what's that good restaurant you talked about?"

West Yellowstone, I say. Wait until you see Slippery Otter Pub and Red Lotus. Maybe we can find an Old Faithful pennant in an antique place. After all the miles and mileage, we're just visiting.

Maybe, in the privilege of moving and running, I've always been a visitor. All of us, after all, are just passing through.

POSTSCRIPT:
POOL OF REVERIE

Approaching the autumn of 2024 (and, we understand, the winter of our lives), Mary Jane and I are going back, again, to the splendiferous northwest corner of Wyoming.

We're booked Into Jackson Lake Lodge in Grand Teton National Park for the first week in October, also the last week of the summer season. The day after we leave, the park and all of Yellowstone NP above it basically will shut down until May 2025. (Jackson, of course, thrives in ski season, and in Yellowstone the Snow Lodge at Old Faithful and highway from the north stay open, for cross-country skiers and snow-shoers and the Sno-Cat and snowmobile crowd and, of most importance, the people doing the hard work. Maintaining, Improving. Answering the call and the calls.)

I am sitting, just now, in an overblown office chair at a lap-top on a desk I assembled myself from a kit, meaning that it's just slightly lopsided and taped together, a Frankenstein. I am also slightly lop-sided and taped together, at least in spirit and life experience. I can also look out the nearest window, in all weathers and seasons, and see the woods, watch birds fly by and sunlight and shadow shift in the trees, watch the sequence of buds and leaves and life and death.

I hear, as always, my father's voice. "One day at a time." Gradual and progressive, or even gradual and regressive. Smother the alarms, skip the theater.

I also can reimagine my last lone walk up the Old Road, the day before I left. Easy, after all my exertions as a runner, to walk the uphill.

Cloudy but bright, a single pronghorn grazing on a far hill, no elk, no bison, no coyotes, no wolves or bear or moose (I never DID see a wolf or bear or moose).

I look ahead, but I also look back at my time in Yellowstone, seeing faces, hearing voices. As I crown the first big hill, I imagine, coming at me, the full retinue: David McElwain from Mississippi and from the Keyser Grill, Michael and Athena and Linnon and Laura and June and John and Ole (Ron) and Jake and James New York and Preacher Bob, from the NPS the benevolent Melanie Moroney and ranger Jennie, the beautiful Veronika from Slovakia (especially her), the concerned woman my age who engineered my escape from Bitterroot, the photographer John Quick from Illinois, and, from the Gallery & Frameworks, Jerry and Christina and also Elenor and Jonie.

Every one of them brought me in, inviting life and learning.

A bad moment with Jonie lingers, On a second day with Jerry and Christina away, she and I are working a bustling show-floor. We had partnered smoothly, sold a lot of stuff, but just then she was ON me, wanting quick action, now, now, NOW! Cash register, mailing table, front displays, back displays, COME ON!

I finally explode, in full view of customers. I can't take this shit! And I say so, in Dad's stentorian voice. Jonie goes cold, crooks a finger, later goes to J & C with a full report. I dropped, she tells them, the f-bomb, surrounded by customers. No, I tell them. I didn't. She never relents. For the remaining days, we barely spoke.

Christina says, later, that I should think of Jonie as Calamity Jane or Belle Starr, a true woman of the west, ready to help at a moment's notice but taking no crap from anybody. When I learned, a few years later, that Jonie had died, I felt that I owed her a debt I couldn't repay. The cliche, I guess, is to pay it forward.

On the Old Road, finally, coming the other way, I see myself. He is not the same man.

In my early youth I read a slew of DC Superman comics, and I was drawn most not by the crime-fighting and dual identities or the newspaper work at the *Daily Planet* or even by the desirable Lois Lane or Lana Lang but by the Fortress of Solitude.

I have come to realize that, as a shy kid volleyed around the country, I stitched together a super suit of my own. Sometimes it might have been pretense and fantasy, but it became a costume for safety and success. Writing stories for newspapers, I quickly embraced the identity of "reporter," facing a few of the famous and a few more people in crisis and, mostly, many men and women just living and working. I was nosing into not only their public personas but also into their private lives, sharing their histories and life-lessons for their scrapbooks and eternity, or at least archives.

I keep a photo, taken from a costume party among friends in Rochester, hosted by artist friend Susan Mandl, of me in a Clark Kent blazer, and someone with red-painted nails is pulling back the blazer to reveal the emblazoned S of a Superman costume.

The costume can become a straitjacket. Through many mid-year moves and losses of friends and familiar surroundings, I had built protective armor. Yellowstone and Gardiner taught me a lasting and still evolving lesson.

I can imagine myself breaking through my shell, built as surely (but not as beautifully) as mollusks build theirs, and I can imagine seeing through the shells of others or, even better, into their central selves.

At root, there is an essential (if complicated) self. Never mind all the nonsense of pseudo psychoanalysis and guaranteed paradigms for living, most with a sales fee. A primary goal in life might be putting pick-up sticks together into an integrated person, central and lasting, simple and coherent in any situation.

The one with integrity.

Through the years before Yellowstone, I had never paused from the incessant me-my-mine and successes and failures and the urgencies and habits and boredom of everyday living, never took the time to SEE. Yellowstone held the key.

Fold up the Super suit, tuck away the gabardine people-pleaser, see and listen to everyone around you, for good or ill. Stand against bullying and greed and up for positive action, personal and shared, preferably face-to-face. Stay open, without quick judgment, to the enormous variety of human experience.

When Jonie or anyone else calls you a liar or, God-knows, anything from the expanding lexicon of pejoratives, take a breath. Take a moment to see that this is not about you; this is about them. They are the performers; you are the audience. You might applaud or boo, but you will not rush the stage or demand your money back. You will, finally, grow up and grow out.

I want, more than anything, to be authentic, but anyone who tries to be authentic is phony. Stop faking and decorating your life, I tell myself. Learn by doing. Learn by seeing. Learn by caring. Fall short, climb back. Reach out,

That's the story, and I'm out of breath. Been good. No whiners.